DATE DUE

JUN 0 8 1995	
JUL 0 6 1995	
SEP 1 4 1995	
OCT 1 2 1995	
JAN 1 1 1996	
SEP 1 7 1996	
DEC 0 7 1999	

Library Store 47-0119 Peel Off Pressure Sensitive

Training Mules
and Donkeys

A Logical Approach to Longears

Training Mules and Donkeys

A Logical Approach to Longears

by Meredith Hodges

Library of Congress Cataloging-in-Publication Data
Hodges, Meredith, 1950-
    Training mules and donkeys / a logical approach to longears / Meredith Hodges.
        p.   cm.
        "Blue ribbon books."
        Includes bibliographical references and index.
        ISBN 0-931866-58-8
        1. Mules — Training.   2. Donkeys — Training.   I. Title.
SF362.H64   1993
798 — dc20   92-9170
                                                                        CIP

Printed in the United States of America

First Edition
9 8 7 6 5 4 3 2

Cover photo by Meredith Hodges
Cover design by Heidi Greenwood Pate
Text design and layout by Dianne Borneman, Shadow Canyon Graphics

ISBN 0-931866-58-8

Little Jack Horner stood in the corner
Eating his oats and hay
Along came a mare, a breed pioneer,
Who wanted her baby to bray!
Said the mare a year later
To Little Jack Horner
The baby you gave me is great
He's loving and loyal
He's smart and he's strong
For another, I just cannot wait.

DEDICATION

*For those who have
shown me clearly
which path to take . . .*

*For my beautiful, intelligent
and magic mules . . .*

*And for the horses and donkeys
who deserve to be treated
like the intelligent and wonderful
creatures that they are!*

Contents

CHAPTER I: PHYSIOLOGICAL AND PSYCHOLOGICAL ATTRIBUTES 1
    Better than the horse out of which he came
    Muscle structure
    Hybrid vigor
    Intelligence
    Psychology approach

CHAPTER II: UNDERSTANDING THE DONKEY 5
    As it pertains to the mule
    Overcoming avoidance behaviors
    Verbal communication
    Don't drill your donkey
    Establishing ground manners
    Attitude of the trainer

CHAPTER III: CARE AND HANDLING OF THE JACK 11
    Natural instincts
    Confinement
    Alternatives to breeding
    Breeding
    Rules for handling

CHAPTER IV: UNDERSTANDING MULE FOALS 15
    The mare's influence
    Child psychology
    Establishing trust
    Maturity and development
    Halter training

CHAPTER V: GROUND MANNERS AND ATTITUDE DEVELOPMENT 19
    Ground work for halter training
    Teaching to lead
    Ground work for grooming
    Establishing trust and communication
    Avoidance behavior

CHAPTER VI: CATCHING THE DIFFICULT MULE 27
    Assessing his attitude
    The approach
    Getting his attention
    Putting on the halter

CHAPTER VII: TEACHING YOUR MULE TO LOAD **33**
    Attention span
    Introduction to obstacles
    Loading the foal
    Loading the difficult mule

CHAPTER VIII: BEGINNING BASIC TRAINING **39**
    Brief introduction to tack
    Lunging on the lead line
    Halter and showmanship
    Leading over and around obstacles

CHAPTER IX: LUNGING YOUR MULE **48**
    Free lunging in the round pen
    Free lunging in tack
    Long lining in the round pen
    Long lining in the open

CHAPTER X: GROUND-DRIVING IN THE ROUND PEN **59**
    Adjusting the bit
    Attaching the long lines
    Use of the lines

CHAPTER XI: GROUND-DRIVING IN THE OPEN **65**
    Introduction to draw reins
    Assessing his aptitude
    Ground-driving patterns
    Introducing the whip
    Ground-driving obstacles

CHAPTER XII: LATERAL WORK ON THE LONG LINES **73**
    Lateral work against the fence
    Lateral work in the open
    Coordinating hands and whip cues
    Practical application

CHAPTER XIII: ADJUSTING YOUR HARNESS **79**
    Check for fit and condition
    Putting on the harness
    Double check for safety

CHAPTER XIV: FINISHING THE DRIVING MULE **87**
    Driving with poles
    Ground-driving in the shafts
    Driving from the cart

CHAPTER XV: JUDGING THE DRIVING MULE **93**
    Manners
    Conditioning
    Way of going
    Appropriateness of turnout
    The reinsman
    Vehicle, harness, and turnout

CHAPTER XVI: TRAINING TO SADDLE **99**
   Preparing to mount
   Mounting
   Round pen review on the lunge line
   Round pen review solo

**CHAPTER XVII: ENGLISH OR WESTERN —
DRESSAGE MEANS "TRAINING"** **107**
   Setting realistic goals
   Addressing good posture and balance
   Saddle differences
   Conditioning your mule
   Sensible training practices

CHAPTER XVIII: PROPER CONDITIONING THROUGH BALANCE **113**
   Avoiding the path to resistance
   Conditioning the athlete
   Sensible training practices

CHAPTER XIX: MOVING OFF OF YOUR LEGS **121**
   Turn on the forehand
   Sidepass the circle
   Slowing his rhythm

CHAPTER XX: REIN BACK **127**
   Avoidance behaviors
   Understanding body mechanics
   Preparing to back
   The cues
   Backing the donkey

CHAPTER XXI: CLARIFYING THE AIDS **133**
   From the mule's standpoint
   Visualization and sensation
   The riding crop
   The serpentine
   Developing the half-halt — rebalancing

CHAPTER XXII: FACILITATING BALANCE AND HARMONY **139**
   Riding without the reins
   "On the bit"
   Balancing over ground poles
   Balancing over cavaletti
   Jumping

CHAPTER XXIII: LATERAL WORK UNDER SADDLE **147**
   Review turn on forehand
   Review lateral wheel
   Leg yield exercises

CHAPTER XXIV: BETTER BALANCE AND LATERAL RESPONSE **153**
   Maximizing use-life
   Spiral circle
   Sidepassing the "T"

CHAPTER XXV: CLARIFYING THE FORWARD/LATERAL CONNECTION 159
Turn-on-the-forehand on the circle
Turn-on-the-haunches
"Fencing" the mule
Backing straight
Getting him "in front of your legs"
Getting him "on the bit"

CHAPTER XXVI: ENHANCING STRENGTH AND MUSCULAR DEVELOPMENT 165
Vertical balance and speed control
Shoulder-in
Lengthening the trot

CHAPTER XXVII: FINE TUNING THE RIDER 171
Principles and philosophy
Physiological and psychological changes
Strengthening body position
Riding without your reins

CHAPTER XXVIII: FINE TUNING THE AIDS 177
Planning course of action
Balancing with your legs
Repetition of the aids

CHAPTER XXIX: ATTITUDES AND USE OF RESTRAINTS 181
Trainer attitude
Response time
Draw reins
Scotch hobble
Face tie

CHAPTER XXX: GROOMING AND CLIPPING FOR SHOW 189
When to clip
Regular grooming and feed
Personalized tack for showing
Rehearsals for organization
Organizing to show
Body clipping and overall grooming

CHAPTER XXXI: RESPONSIBILITIES TO THE VETERINARIAN AND FARRIER 201
Making a good impression
Common professional complaints
Preparing your mule
Client complaints
Mutual respect

Glossary 207
References 217
Index 219

Foreword

When my husband Paul and I first started the group known as the American Donkey and Mule Society, we realized that the main problem we had to face was the fact that information on donkeys and mules was almost nonexistent. The verbal knowledge that had been passed along through the generations was dying out and could not in any case be easily shared with the new public, which at this time was beginning to get seriously interested in these animals.

Oddly enough, books on donkeys started appearing on the market in moderate quantities after this time as a new club, oriented only for donkeys, came into being in England — at about the same time that ADMS started in the United States. At this time, however, there was only one actual book on the subject of mules, and it had been written about one hundred years ago! The staff at ADMS started reprinting *A Treatise on the Mule* by Harvey Riley, written in 1869, and were glad to have anything with which to help people.

I still know of only three general-purpose mule books in print, which means that *Training Mules and Donkeys: A Logical Approach to the Longears* by Meredith Hodges will fill a place that has been vacant for many years.

There are thousands of mule lovers in the United States who feel that they do not know how to train their mules or donkeys and who, in despair, put them into the hands of trainers who do not understand their particular character, and who proceed to ruin animals that have the potential to be safe and loving companions for the next forty years. It is everyone's hope that this book will help those individuals, or their trainers, to understand mules and donkeys and to handle them correctly.

All of us at the American Donkey and Mule Society hope that this book will improve the lot of an animal that is very popular and that could be far more popular if correct training methods were applied so that everyone who wants one could have a beautiful, well-mannered, well-trained, modern mule.

— Betsy Hutchins
Co-Founder, American Donkey and Mule Society

Preface

The information on donkeys and mules has been sketchy to say the least over the past twenty years, and the information about training longears has been even less. For twenty years, I had to rely on my knowledge of horse training, coupled with my experience as a psychiatric technician. Oddly enough, it was my psychiatric counseling experience that actually gave me the key to training mules and donkeys. Basically, "you can catch more flies with sugar than you can with vinegar," and, "a little patience and understanding go a long way." Looking upon my mules as children along the path of life enabled me to find the path of least resistance to success with them. It has allowed me to maximize my enjoyment of these wonderful companions!

It was exciting for me to achieve so easily with my mules by taking a few simple ideas into consideration. I have recorded the concepts that were especially successful and compiled them into this book, because I wish to share the knowledge that has brought about *my* satisfaction and success in working with longears.

There are times when training longears can seem like a hopelessly frustrating job if you do not consider the dynamics of longears thought and behavior. When mules are only two and three years old, you are convinced that you may kill them because of their youthful antics! But treat your mule as if he were a precocious child, and the less desired behaviors will tend to subside over time. Allow patience and understanding to govern punitive actions, and realize that your longear's attention span will afford more timely obedience at a later time.

Knowing some simple psychology and training techniques will help you toward a more enjoyable and rewarding experience with your longears and will afford you a lot less frustration than I suffered during the training process. I would like to see others experience the same joy that I have at last found with my longears today!

Acknowledgements

I would like to thank my mother, Joyce Doty, for giving me the chance to begin my career with mules at the Windy Valley Mule Ranch in Healdsburg, California. Thanks to my father, Charles M. Schulz, who gave me the courage to follow my dreams. Thanks to my daughter, Dena, for her support and inspiration throughout the years of hardship and frustration.

Thank you to Paul and Betsy Hutchins of the American Donkey and Mule Society for providing a sound foundation for longears from which to grow and for their encouragement and support along the way! Thank you Richard Schrake for introducing me to a fun and resistance-free way of winning. Thank you Melinda Weatherford, United States Dressage Federation and United States Combined Training Association instructor/coordinator, for showing me what hundreds of years of horsemanship is all about and for the friendships that have since blossomed.

Thank you Steve Schwartzenberger for giving us our first World Championship in Reining! Thank you Jack Patterson for paving the road to excellence in driving. Thank you to Newt and Opal Elsdon, who have always been there for us at our world show competition at Bishop Mule Days. Thank you Judy Rose of Sweetwater Stables, Pat Mitchell of Mitchell's Mules, and Gail Altieri, world class competitors who have loyally and enthusiastically supported us throughout the years. Thank you Fran and Larry Howe of the Bitterroot Mule Company for friendship and comraderie through thick and thin in support of longears!

Thank you to the mules and donkeys in my life who have taught me humility, unending patience, and understanding. And a heartfelt thank you to Betty Jo McKinney for acting on the need for a book such as this!

Diane Hunter McElvain and Grace from Africa.

CHAPTER I

Physiological and Psychological Attributes

Across the United States and around the world, mules are exhibiting their exceptional athletic ability as we give them the opportunities to perform in many diverse situations. Many people, however, still do not understand why the mule is as capable as he is. There are definite physical and psychological reasons for these outstanding abilities. It has been said that he is more athletic than the horse out of which he came, and the reason is really quite simple. The mule not only inherits the best qualities from that horse but also inherits the best qualities from his sire, the jack, who is responsible for the mule's muscular structure, his strength, and his intelligence.

The muscular structure of a mule is noticeably different from that of a horse. His body is covered with masses of long, smooth muscle, while the horse has more differentiated masses of muscle. The most apparent example of this difference is seen in the chest of the mule. While the horse has two distinct groups of muscles, the mule's chest is composed of one wide mass of muscle closely resembling a turkey's breast. This muscular mass greatly enhances the mobility of the area that it surrounds. Another example is found in the mule's hindquarters, where the long, wide, smooth muscles enable the mule to kick forward, backward, and to the side, and even scratch the top of his head with a hindfoot should he so desire. Horses cannot do this because of their smaller, bulkier masses of muscle. The difference is similar to that between a dancer and a weight lifter; the longer, smooth muscles are more conducive to athletic performance in speed and agility.

Given the physical structure to perform more diversely, the mule is given by his sire the strength to withstand extended use of these muscles. Try to budge an unwilling horse and an unwillingly donkey that is half the size of the horse, and you will realize the incredible strength of the donkey! This is not stubbornness, but unbelievable vigor. This vigor is passed on to the mule, adding to his superiority over the horse in strength and endurance.

1

Above: Lucky Three Mae C.J. and Ciji — matching pairs.
Left: Little Jack Horner: working trot.

Left: Lucky Three Sundowner preparing for lessons.
Below: Lucky Three Sundowner, 1984 World Champion Bridle Reined Mule.

This combination of an agile muscular structure and incredible strength could be quite dangerous were it not for the increased intelligence of the animal. Donkeys seem to have a genuine concern for health and happiness, and the mule inherits this from his sire. Donkeys and mules have been labeled "stubborn" for centuries, but given the sometimes foolish expectations that humans have put on them, you can hardly blame them for not complying with our wishes. It is not stubbornness that causes an overloaded donkey to stop dead in his tracks to rest his body, but rather common sense and a strong desire for self-preservation. Would a sensible human being deliberately pack more than he could carry comfortably, then continue a hike until he dropped from heat and exhaustion? Can you call him stubborn if he does not? Certainly not! You must say that he is being sensible in his desire for self-preservation. The same applies in any potentially life-threatening situation. When crossing water, for example, the donkey does not possess the visual depth perception of humans; therefore, he is only being cautious when he refuses to step readily into water. He needs time to evaluate the situation and determine its threat to his existence. It is his health with which he is concerned!

Donkeys, as intelligent as they are, also seem to know that humans are not always concerned with what is really best for them, yet donkeys always give humans the opportunity to convince them. Donkeys have a natural social attraction to humans, and, when treated with patience, kindness, and understanding, they learn to trust and obey. If they are treated with pain and abuse, however, they are not likely to comply with our wishes; anger and irrationality do not perpetuate happiness and self-preservation. Ask yourself: Do you perform more willingly when someone is kind and supportive, or when someone is angry and abusive? The answer is simple. The intelligence of these donkeys is no accident and this intelligence, strength, and muscular structure, coupled with the gentle disposition and other fine qualities of the horse, make for a superior animal in the mule.

As we learn more about these long-eared animals, we also learn more about ourselves. These animals seem to bring out the best in all of us who associate with them. Now, more than ever, donkey and mule farms and clubs are thriving throughout the world, sharing ideas and benefiting from each other because of the existence of these truly amazing, long-eared diplomats.

Young mules have very intimate social behaviors and many private conversations with each other . . . often about you!

Little Jack Horner fully understands the aids for the leg yield.

CHAPTER II

Understanding the Donkey

Before you begin to train your mule, it is important to understand the psychology of the donkey as it pertains to the mule. If you train donkeys, you need to know that there are differences between the donkey and the mule that will affect your training techniques. Inherently, the horse can be mastered, or controlled, relatively easily. Inherently, donkeys can be coerced but not necessarily controlled like the horse. The mule, being one-half donkey and one-half horse, falls somewhere in between; therefore, it is important to consider both horse and donkey psychology when training the mule.

There is little difference in technique or approach in training horses and mules, provided that you are patient and understanding and that you employ a good reward system. The major difference between these two equines is their ability to tolerate negative reinforcement, or punishment. The mule, being part donkey, does not tolerate punitive action very well unless he is fully aware that the fault is his own and the punishment is fair. For instance, you ask for a canter lead and your mule keeps trotting; one good smack with the whip, or one good gig with the spurs, is *negative reinforcement* that will bring about the desired response. However, more than one or two good smacks or gigs can cause either a runaway or an extremely balky animal. This kind of resistance comes from the donkey and requires a much different approach if you are training donkeys. This type of resistance is more easily overcome in mules because of their horse nature. Mules therefore are easier to train than donkeys.

It is the innate desire of all humans to control their own lives, both emotional and environmental. When they cannot, they become panicked and confused about their situation. They doubt themselves, their abilities, and their self-worth. If people do not maintain a sense of humor about situations and factors that cannot be controlled, they are doomed to depression and failure. Horses can be controlled, and so can mules, for the most part. It is my experience, however, that donkeys are controlled only when they so desire.

Donkeys are affectionate, amicable characters and possess such a sensitive nature that you would think punishment a real deterrent from bad behavior. When you punish a donkey, however, you will find a tough hide and an unbelievable avoidance behavior that can cause more resistance than it's worth! And if this isn't enough, if you do punish your donkey for a certain deed, the next time he even comes close to that same action, he may anticipate your punishment and go straight to the avoidance behavior before actually making the mistake. For this reason, it is better to try to ignore the mistakes and to focus on the successes and reward them with lots of praise.

If you encounter resistance to a part of your training program, and that part is not necessary for your final objectives, just drop it and go on to the next step. Donkeys get impatient when you don't "get to the point." So, if you want to ride your donkey, put on the saddle and the bridle, put him in a small pen, get right on, and go! He might benefit from a little ground-driving first, but in my experience, it doesn't matter which comes first. If you are considerate and polite to your donkey, he will generally enjoy giving you a ride.

The only lesson that I state clearly is "Whoa." Turning the donkey into a tight circle seems to accomplish this as well as anything, but you need the correct gear to do it. He should be outfitted in a plain snaffle bridle and English or Western saddle. Use spurs, crops, and draw reins when needed. When I first tried lunging my donkey, he either stood stock-still or ran off; when I ground-drove him, he took off so quickly that he yanked me to my knees and dragged me through the dirt. When I rode him, we ran from one end of the pen to the other until he got tired. Then we stopped and I had to coax him back to the barn with a bucket of grain! Any "normal" person probably would have given up, but I loved my donkey and was convinced that he could be trained like a mule.

The first step in training donkeys is to realize that they are not like mules and horses; therefore, it will take a lot longer to get the desired responses. It took me four months to get my jack to lope one complete circle on

command! Don't get impatient. Just be persistent and maintain your sense of humor. After all, wouldn't *you* chuckle at someone who was having as much trouble with a donkey? Donkeys can act so incredibly dumb, but they can always make an ass out of any trainer. How dumb can that really be?

A few simple tricks and some basic knowledge of donkey behavior will help you through difficult times in donkey training. A donkey uses his head and neck for avoidance behavior, and because a donkey is strong, control of the head and neck must be voluntary. A simple pull on the rein does not always work. For this reason, you need to use other turning aids. Spurs can be helpful. When turning, give an indication of direction with your direct rein, then back it up more strongly with your leg on the opposite side, asking him to move away from the leg pressure (or spur). It is easier to turn his body first rather than to turn his head and neck and hope that his body follows. If using spurs is not enough, tie a paper sack to the end of a short whip and use this on the side of your donkey's head and neck to cause him to turn in conjunction with the use of your legs. Do not hit your donkey any harder than it takes to turn him, and be careful not to hit any sensitive areas such as his eyes and ears. After a couple of times, he will see the bag coming and will turn on his own. Once he learns this, he will pay closer attention to your direct rein and your legs; then you can move on to more conventional training methods.

You can use this same technique to train your "Whoa." Use your whip to turn him into a tight circle until he stops, then reward him! One of the most effective forms of resistance used by donkeys and mules is to "lean" on the bridle and run off. Generally, if there is nothing to lean on, they will run only as far as their natural instinctive flight pattern dictates, which isn't very far. Therefore, your rein indications must be light and quick, giving no chance for pulling. Your donkey must feel free to respond on his own accord. He must believe that it was *his* idea and not the result of human will. You need to do as *little as possible* to get the desired response. If he does run off, don't fight it; just ride him out until he stops, reward him for stopping, then go back and try again. During breeding season, I had thirty runaways before I could get my jack to trot one figure-eight! Patience and persistence finally paid off. In ground-work, use draw reins to give yourself some leverage. If he does start to run, you can then pull one rein hard enough to bring his head around to the tight circle. This will disengage his hindquarters and curb the forward motion.

It is extremely important to establish verbal communication with your donkey. From the beginning, get into the habit of identifying every movement of your donkey, and always use the same commands: Walk, Trot, Canter, Back, Gee, Haw, Gee-over, Haw-over, Gee-around, and Haw-around ("over" meaning a side pass and "around" meaning a complete turn on the haunches). Success in verbal communication is most prevalent in donkeys. They might ignore your hands and legs but seem to listen to your voice when all else has failed. This becomes particularly important when dealing with canter leads and flying changes and when defining each side of your donkey's body.

Don't drill your donkey! If your donkey has almost done what you ask, be satisfied and ask no more that day. He will more than likely do it better next time if you don't push. Take it from one who has spent four hours trying to repeat one move correctly only to have to quit as a failure! I was in tears, but my jack wasn't bothered at all. The next day he went back and did it correctly the first try. All I managed to do by drilling him was cause myself a lot of anger and frustration. A donkey needs to be able to perform in his own time and space. You may as well be patient, or he may never try to please.

Don't work your donkey too often. It takes time to convince a donkey that being with you is more fun. Have short periods of good times together at first. Keep your lessons short, easy, and fun. Soon he will be looking for you to take him out and will learn to please you willingly.

Donkeys are often pushy and try to walk all over you if you let them. Be firm about ground manners in halter and assert your dominance over your donkey. He will then respect you. Be definite with your donkey on the lead. When you stand still, so should he; when you walk, so should he (right at your shoulder). Always have him stop at gates and doorways and allow you to pass through first. If he gets pushy, deter him with a quick smack to the side of his muzzle. Then reward him quickly for complying to alleviate any fear.

I have learned to train donkeys with the help of my own Little Jack Horner. He has taught me much over the years, and I hope that I can pass on this information to the rest of you frustrated donkey trainers. Bear in mind, the first five years can be disheartening if you compare them to training progress with a horse or a mule. In time, if you maintain a good sense of humor and a fair attitude, your donkey will begin to understand and the training will become easier and more rewarding. The donkey will never forget what you teach him regardless of how many days pass between lessons. If you are fair, polite, and honest in your training, the donkey will eventually learn what you ask and will be willing to perform. The donkey is the master of his own fate, and all that trainers can do is ask. It is the donkey that will ultimately decide. Even the most well-trained donkey will have his days or moments. Be fair and understand that this is the way of the world for all of us, and a bad day does not a bad donkey make!

Little Jack Horner is now nine years old. When he was three, we spent many long days on walk, trot, canter, back, circles, and side passes. Those days turned into three years before I got an acceptable Pleasure Class go from him. Since then, he has learned to spin, to slide fifteen feet into a stop, to do all kinds of complex trail obstacles, to perform flying lead changes, to jump controlled over three-foot-plus fences, and to lengthen the trot in harness. Only during the last year has he performed these feats consistently. Still, I must admit that I really don't control him. I can only ask. It is ultimately his decision if we are to perform today; tomorrow could be an entirely different story. But whatever the story, keep smiling, be happy, and don't worry! Your donkey will generally give you what you deserve.

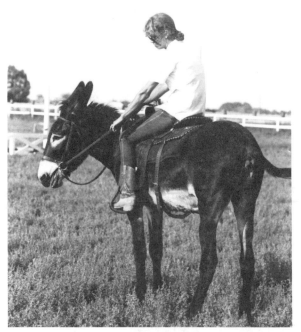

Lucky Three Serendipity: Donkeys tend to lean into direct pressure from both reins at once. Therefore, it is important to get your donkey to give laterally to the bit for more control.

Pull, release, pull, release, until your donkey allows you to pull his nose around to your knee easily. Do this exercise from a standstill at first.

When he gives easily at the standstill, try the same exercise at the walk, and don't stop pulling and releasing until he comes to a complete halt and gives with his head. While you are pulling and releasing, give the verbal command to "Whoa."

When he gives easily and halts from the walk, you can move on to the trot the same way. He will eventually associate the verbal command with the rein pulling and will learn to stop. As he gets more proficient, he will eventually learn to stop with a squeeze-release on both reins and the verbal command to "Whoa."

Obstacles such a logs, bridges, and tires also help your donkey to learn to negotiate his own body movements with your shifts of body weight. Slow conditioning of his muscles will help him to carry you more effectively and without fear.

Time, patience, and *good food* will help your donkey overcome his fear of strange obstacles. Your first attempt at an obstacle will often bring success if you approach it slowly and patiently.

Fran Howe and Bitterroot Mule Company's farm sire, Blue Zebulon. *Joan S. Byrne Photography.*

CHAPTER III

Care and Handling of the Jack

A donkey jack can be your best friend or your worst enemy. Because he is a donkey, he possesses all of those wonderful characteristics unique to donkeys: intelligence, strength, easy maintenance, suitability for many equine sports, and, most important, an innate affectionate attitude. Nevertheless, he is still an instinctual male, often governed by hormones. When nature takes over, the jack's conscious thought is greatly diminished, and he can become hazardous to your health. The jack's aggressiveness is often masked by his sedate, affectionate attitude. This belligerence can arise in a split second and cause the jack to do more damage than a stallion. Usually there is an awkwardness or indecisiveness in an agitated stallion that will allow you time to get out of the way. But the jack reacts strongly, swiftly, and right on target, allowing no time for retreat. By keeping a few simple principles in mind, you can greatly reduce your chances of injury when handling jacks.

Keep your jack in a comfortable atmosphere. Jacks can be great worriers, especially about their mares and jennets. It is ideal to keep the jack well out of sight and smell of the females but not always practical. If he must be near females, make sure that he has a roomy area free of refuse and debris and adequately fenced. The fence should be high enough to discourage leaning over the top and strong enough to bear the jack's weight on impact. It should have no protrusions that could cause him injury. If females or other animals are present, the jack may run back and forth along the fence and catch his head on any such protrusion. Hot wires used alone are not sufficient. If your jack becomes frightened, he could run through an electric wire before he even knows that it is there. He will be calmer and more manageable if he is given a clean, comfortable area where his limits are defined clearly.

Spend time with your jack. Use him for more than just breeding. This will give him an alternative purpose in life that can diffuse his obsession with females. Many jack owners use their jacks for riding and driving, as well as for breeding. This is an excellent plan. If you lack the time or inclination to use your jack this way and wish to use him exclusively for breeding, at least take a few minutes, two or three

11

Little Jack Horner proudly displays his Merit of Breeding and Versatility Hall of Fame awards from the American Donkey and Mule Society, proving that donkeys can do it, too!

days a week, to work on halter training and manageability. Teach him to walk, to trot, to whoa, and to stand still on the lead. During these sessions, be positive and relaxed and emphasize your rapport with him rather than his performance. Give him something to look forward to besides females. Be his friend. When you take the time to train him properly at halter, you will enhance his obedience, even during breeding.

When you use your jack for breeding, develop a routine that he can count on every time. Then, when you are not breeding him, do things a little differently. This will help him to decide clearly how to behave. For instance, when Little Jack Horner is bred here at the Lucky Three Ranch, the mare is prepared first. Then I go to his stall, ask him to step back (which is very important to prevent him from running you down), put on his halter, and run the lead shank under his chin (it isn't advisable to go through the mouth, because he could bite you inadvertently). I ask him to Whoa (allowing me out the door first), then lead him to the breeding area and tie him up. Just from the stall to the breeding area, the jack has learned not to be pushy and aggressive toward the handler.

When in the breeding area, the jack must be taught patience and obedience. If the mare is left to stand just out of reach until the jack is ready to breed, the jack may become anxious and unruly. To clarify your intentions to him, you can take the cloth that you used to clean the mare and place it near the jack's nose, allowing him a good, strong scent of the mare. This will ready your jack for breeding more quickly and decrease his anxiety time substantially. If your jack is indifferent, his interest in the female may actually be increased, and this may shorten the breeding process time. The fact

Diane Hunter, Cliff Rich, and driver with Red Man, at Bishop Mule Days, 1984.

that you brought him the scent allows the jack to believe that it is your decision when to breed and not his and that he must remain obedient.

Let him cover the mare only when he is fully ready. Just to be on the safe side, either muzzle your jack or use a dropped noseband (fit snugly) while breeding; this will prevent biting injuries to you and the mare. When he is done, make him stand quietly behind the mare while you rinse him off. Allow him that last sniff to the mare's behind, then take him back to his stall (or pen) and ask him to stand while you remove the halter. Then let him go. That last sniff seems to be an assertion of his act and of his manhood. If you try to lead him away before he sniffs, he might not want to come with you. Doing things routinely will allow your jack to relax and use the manners that he has learned.

It is best that menstruating women not go near a jack or stallion. The woman may be perceived as an object of the animal's hormonal drive, and she may be subject to great bodily harm, particularly in the case of the jack.

When you are around a jack, always be alert and know what he is doing. A jack can be the most adorable, lovable, obedient guy in the world. You must realize, though, that his natural instincts can arise at *any* time, and even though he may not mean to, he can hurt you severely just the same! When you are observing a jack from the other side of the fence, realize that he can come over the top, teeth bared. Don't *ever* turn your back to him! When putting on or taking off any headgear, watch your fingers carefully! When a jack knows that the shank or bit is coming, he often opens his jaws to meet it, and your fingers can easily get in the way. If you keep these basic safety factors in mind, you and your jack can have a long, happy, rewarding relationship!

Little Jack Horner.

Blue Baron.

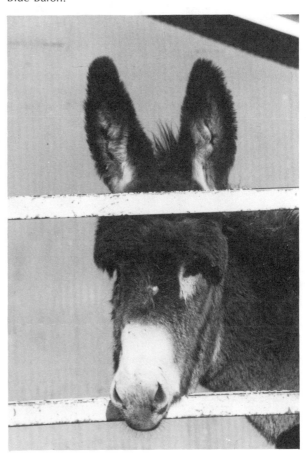

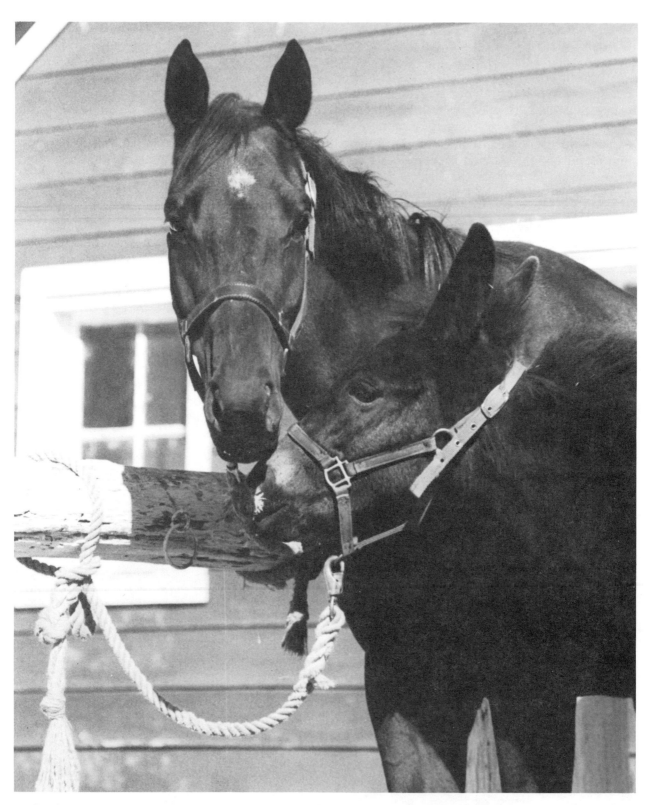

Lucky Three Midnight Victory with dam, Vinesse (American Trakehner Association #ORB-B-M678).

CHAPTER IV

Understanding Mule Foals

If ever there are equines born with a natural affinity for human beings, they are mules and donkeys. Raising your mule or donkey foal to accept humans can be a relatively easy affair if you remember a few simple points.

First, the foal learns a great deal from his dam. He will spend the first five to six months with her, mostly alone. If you wish your foal to be friendly and cooperative, be sure that your foal's dam is friendly and cooperative. A mule or donkey foal from a sour or uncooperative dam eventually learns her avoidance behavior, despite his deeper instinct to be amicable. For instance, if your mare or jennet leaves when you approach, the foal at her side eventually learns to leave as well, whether he is truly frightened or not. This behavior can carry over into adulthood. This is not to say that you cannot teach both the mare and foal to be more amicable—it's just that you will need more time and patience. This brings me to my next point.

Mule foals are not much different from our own human babies in their emotional needs. They need lots of attention, love, guidance, and praise if they are to evolve into loving, cooperative, confident adults. In an effort to get these youngsters trained, we often forget that they are still children. If expected to fulfill too many adult responsibilities too quickly, the mule foal can become overwhelmed, frustrated, and resistant. This is why I try to give my foals plenty of time to be "children." At the same time, I play games with them that will help them to prepare for adulthood without imposing adult expectations.

The first component of developing a well-adjusted adult mule is to establish a routine that will give your mule foal a sense of security and trust in you. Having a definite feeding schedule can help considerably. If you take a few minutes each morning and evening to feed his dam, then to scratch and pet him, your foal will associate you with a very pleasurable experience. If his dam is busy eating, she will be less likely to run off with the foal. If your animals are on pasture, a short visit once, or better, twice a day with a special ration of treats will accomplish the same objective.

Gary Hodges and Lucky Three Firestorm. Baby mules always enjoy a good game of tag!

Once you have developed a routine, pay close attention to your foal's likes and dislikes. Each foal is different and has definite ways in which he likes to be touched and definite places on his body from which he derives pleasure. By touching, stroking, and scratching him all over his body, you can easily discover his preferences. If he expresses a dislike for any particular touch, either modify or discontinue it. Once a foal discovers the pleasure of your hands on his body, moving down his legs usually poses little or no problem. When he has grown accustomed to your touch on his legs, he will allow you to pick up his feet for short periods of time. All that I have mentioned thus far should be done *while the mule is free and unconstrained.* It is *his* choice to stay with you! If he is tied or constrained in any manner, he can become tense and frightened and you can be perceived as a threat. This produces resistance.

Mules are about a year or more behind horses in their overall development. For this reason, it is unadvisable to begin formal training in their second year. At two years of age, your mule is still a rambunctious child and will not necessarily take kindly to being restrained. Because he is not that physically developed either, his resistance could injure him both mentally and physically. It is better to use your imagination and teach only the simplest activities at this age.

Mule foals love to play games, and they have a tremendous sense of humor. One of my mules'

favorite games is tag. Once your foal figures out that you mean him no harm and that you wish to give him pleasure, he will begin to follow you, butting his nose against you. To teach him to play tag, just pet him a couple of times, then turn and trot away a few steps. Turn again and encourage him to follow. It won't take him long to figure out the game. This is especially fun for foals that do not have other foals for playmates. If your foal gets a little strong and jumps at you or on you, tap your hand on his nose and give a firm "No." This will define the limitations of the game and he will develop no

Lucky Three Mercedes and Pantera (foal).

bad habits. Directly after you discipline him, be sure to let him know that you have punished his indiscretion and now intend to forget it. Encourage him to continue playing.

When your mule gets a little older and is ready to be halter broken, you can use your pleasurable status with him to your advantage. Halter him and tie him to the fence. About every fifteen to thirty minutes, come to him, untie him, and ask him to follow you. If he refuses, just tie him up again and return later. If he comes with you, even if it is only for a few steps, take off the halter and play for awhile before you leave. This will maintain your pleasure status with your mule while he learns matters that he will need as an adult.

When he leads fairly well, add the game of obstacles. Any chance that you get, take your foal with you and discover "things" together on the lead line. Let him know that everything is alright and that you will protect him if necessary. Put yourself between the obstacle and the mule if he becomes frightened, and let him have plenty of time to investigate the situation. When he does show interest, encourage him to come forward and investigate further, then pet him and praise him when he touches the obstacle with his nose. If he learns to stop and investigate scary obstacles in this way as a youngster, he will be more apt to stop and trust your judgment as an adult.

When you handle your mule foal, always be sure to give him time to relax and accept a situation—and he probably will. Do not try to force a situation. He will be happy to oblige you with more resistance than you ever imagined! Never get in a hurry—it's faster not to! And remember, you can catch more flies with sugar than you can with vinegar. Go out there and have a good time with your little long-eared pal. He'll be glad to be your best friend if you learn to be his best friend.

Lucky Three Firestorm rolling. "Come on, Mom, let's play! If Mom won't play, a good roll will suffice!"

Mules enjoy a clean and healthy environment. When their surroundings are comfortable, their minds are more healthy and receptive.

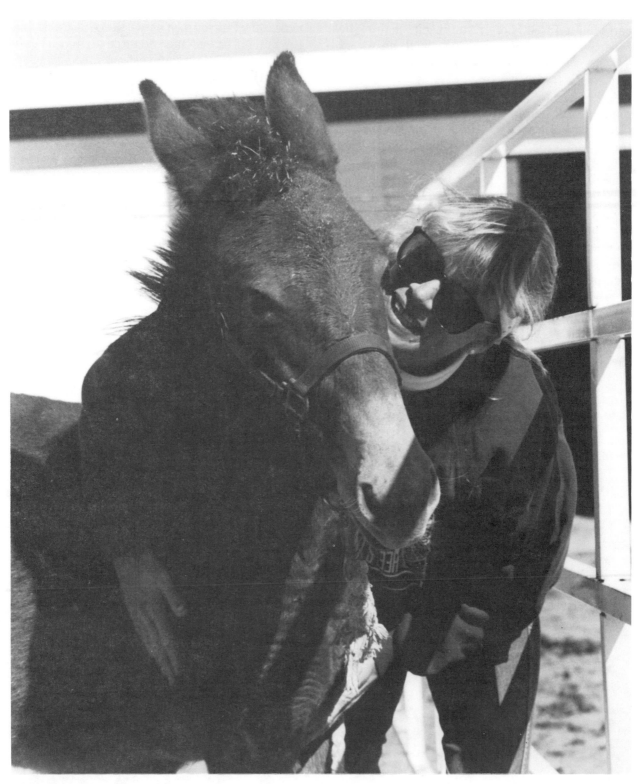

Lucky Three Felicia's Fairytale is quite pleased with herself!

CHAPTER V

Ground Manners and Attitude Development

When and how should you begin to train a young mule? What kinds of behaviors can you expect? Mules, like horses, enjoy the company of their own kind, but they also enjoy time with their human companions. Too much leisure time can become a bore for a mule; he enjoys new activities provided that they are pleasurable for him.

You can begin training your mule as a new foal by gently scratching and massaging him all over his body, legs, and head. Beginning in this way will desensitize him slowly and easily, laying a good foundation for handling him the rest of his life. Be careful not to frighten him; make your movements slow and deliberate. Stay near "Mother" during these sessions; if she is the overprotective type, tie her up nearby.

When the mule foal has learned to relax during these massages, you can introduce the halter. Just put it on and leave your foal loose to get the feel of it. Be sure that he is in an enclosure where the halter will not get hung up on some object. He can wear his halter all day, but it is best to remove it at night when you cannot watch him. Removing the halter at night will automatically cause you to adjust the halter properly each day. The head of a baby mule grows quickly, and a halter left on too long can become tight, causing indentations in the nose and irritation to the hair and skin. Also, by putting it on and taking it off each day, he will become used to being caught. This will allow you to catch him more easily later. When he is no longer bothered by the halter, it is time to proceed to the next step.

Begin teaching him to lead by simply tying him to a stout post for awhile each day. At this point, I must caution you not to use this technique on horse foals because they do not have the "sense" of a mule and may wind up injuring themselves. The mule will learn not to pull away from the lead rope. I generally leave the babies alone for one-half hour at first; then I walk to the post where one is tied and wait for him to slacken the lead rope before I release him. Repeat this procedure for as many days as it takes before he does not pull back at all.

When he stands quietly, begin taking steps with him. Take the lead rope in your hand and try walking backward, facing him. When he leads easily, you can turn around. If he pulls away, tie him up again and leave for about fifteen minutes, then come back and try again. Halter breaking this way allows the mule to consider what you are asking of him. It also helps you to control your own temper. No one has ever really won a war with a mule!

To add variety to these sessions, you may want to start using a soft brush on the baby's body and begin picking up his feet. At this point, he is still a manageable size, and it is to your advantage to get those feet under control!

When your mule is a weanling, you will become his substitute mother, and he will be willing to follow you just about anywhere that you choose to go. Mules love attention, and with a little creativity, you can make your training sessions so pleasurable that your mule will not even realize that he is being trained. For instance, in advanced halter training, don't limit yourself to the same area each day; take a walk! Mules enjoy scenery as much as you do. Besides, by exposing him to many new objects and activities at this stage, you will diminish the number of "spooks" that he will encounter later. He will also learn to handle his fear better through his love and trust in you.

During the walks with your mule, talk to him about what you are doing with him. When you walk, ask him to "Walk;" when you stop, ask him to "Whoa." Tell him when he is being good, and when he does not comply, just ignore him for a few minutes, then try again. By establishing verbal communication with your mule, future lessons will come a lot more easily. Introduce him to as many new situations as you can. By dressing him up as Santa Claus at Christmas, you get him used to a lot of variety and also allow him to be an active participant in creating fond memories for you and your family. Mules are like small children, and when they are treated as such, they grow up with more curiosity than fear and with a love of their master that enables them to always give their best.

In spite of their love, however, at times your young mule simply will not wish to comply. Remember—he is just a baby, and some of his antics will be undesirable. These problems do not reflect the overall disposition of your mule and usually will dissipate over time.

What of the baby that will let you catch him easily only part of the time? On the days when he does not wish to comply, you will probably sense that he is toying with you. When baby mules are confident in their owner's love, they enjoy playing all sorts of games. If you are pressed for time and must catch baby immediately, simply tie his mother in a corner and wait for him to join her. Then move in quietly for the catch. When catching baby, get one arm around the neck and the other hand on his tail. To apply the halter, back him into a wall. This will enable you to release the hold on the tail and free your hand to put on the halter. If you have more time, just ignore baby for awhile and lavish his dam with attention until baby returns and begs you to pay attention to him. And, being a mule, he will return! This is the preferred method, because it allows the mule to make the decision for himself. Then he can be amply rewarded for being so good, even if it takes a little time.

At this early age, baby mules like to nip, and sometimes they will even take a kick at you despite your patience and careful training. If your mule gets too rough, give him a firm swat with the flat of your hand and a firm "No" to let him know of your disapproval. If he nips, carefully "spank" him on the side of his mouth and say "No." If he kicks, and you can reach him, "spank" him on the rear firmly and say "No." If you cannot reach him after he kicks, say "No" firmly, then turn all of your attention away from him and do not give him any more until he quiets down and complies with your standard of communication.

Do not get into a punitive situation with your mule. Babies are unable to really comprehend why their natural instincts are being construed as bad behavior. Always try to set him up for success so that he can be rewarded. As he approaches his second year, your mule generally will begin to calm down considerably

Halter breaking can be fun when you make a game of it! Felicia, Lindy, and Vicki, from Lucky Three Ranch.

Brayer Hill Razzle Dazzle, only two days old, from Brayer Hill Farm, Boyd, Texas.

and his attention span will be much longer. At this time, he will begin to understand the rights and wrongs of his behavior in relation to you.

When mules are concentrating, they lay back their ears. This is not an exhibition of disapproval as it is in horses. If a mule is genuinely displeased, he will lay his ears positively flat back, and the look in his eyes will reflect his displeasure. Baby mules love to play "chase" with humans, laying back their ears and nipping at the person's back. If your mule does this, do not be alarmed; just keep your wits about you when you play. If your mule gets too aggressive, stop and face him, then say "No." When he complies and settles down, lavish him with hugs and scratches, then go on and play

some more. This will subtly teach your young mule that he must learn to control his behavior if he is to have the pleasure of your company.

Young mules are sociable, lovable animals. They do have natural instincts that can be injurious to humans, but these can be modified with loving discipline. The beginning years with your baby mule provide a great time for establishing a solid, loving, working relationship. This is really a time for minimal training with maximal observation and positive interaction. This is the time to *set the stage* for learning and to enjoy all of the cute, entertaining little antics of your baby mule. Proper attitude development now will carry him into an enjoyable and successful future.

On your approach, your baby mule will, no doubt, pull back first.

Speak in a quiet, soothing voice, and encourage him to come forward. Do not try to force him.

If he seems a little tense, stroke him gently with reassuring words.

He may become suddenly frightened and again show resistance. If he does, just step back, allow him to settle, then try again.

This time, stay in position and ask him to come to you for the petting and reassurance.

He will eventually take that step toward you and allow the rope to slacken. Do this exercise until he no longer flies back on the rope.

Lucky Three "Jubilee": When brushing your foal, make sure to use a soft brush and start at the front, working toward the rear.

Pick up his feet only as long as he will allow easily. As he gets used to this, he will allow you to pick them up for longer periods of time.

When your mule is comfortable about your approach while he is tied, you can think about actually leading him.

Give a slight tug on the lead and hold the slack while encouraging him with your soft voice to come forward.

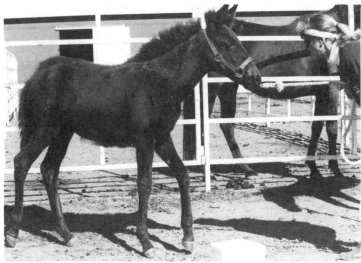

Sometimes it helps if you put your face on his level. You are less threatening to him if he perceives that you are no larger than himself, and he will come forward easily.

A gentle kiss on the nose and gentle strokes are really praise enough for the foal.

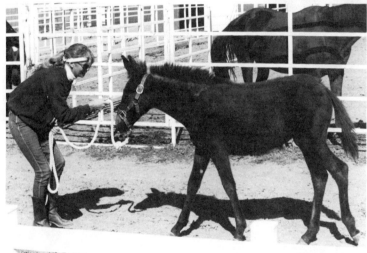

Starting a foal leading is less threatening to him if you first walk backward, coaxing him to come while keeping the lead rope slackened.

When he has overcome his initial fear, you can turn around and he should follow you more easily. If he does pull away, try to stand your ground as a post and be as nonthreatening as possible.

Lucky Three Felicia's Fairytale. "Look, Ma, an extension!"

CHAPTER VI

Catching the Difficult Mule

Not all mules are fortunate enough to be raised so that they gain confidence and trust. These mules need to be approached as if they were young foals just beginning their training. To begin their training, you must first be able to catch them.

There is probably nothing more infuriating than having a mule that you can't catch easily when you wish. The young mule that has been introduced to the halter at an early age can pose a problem, just like the mule that has had no halter training at all. The reasons for their evasive behavior and the intensity of resistance are different, however. The mule that has been handled will periodically attempt to assert his dominance over you with a playful yet evasive attitude, while the mule that has not been handled will react out of fear and suspicion. You can deal with both of these mules in the same manner to produce positive results, but the one reacting fearfully could become aggressive and potentially dangerous because he feels a need to protect himself from you. The one that has been handled will seldom be as aggressive. He may kick at you, but he probably won't touch you intentionally because he has learned that this is bad manners. Be careful, because the fearful and aggressive mule will most likely connect with his target!

When a mule is being evasive, it is fairly obvious that his attention is not totally on you, and for him to be obedient, he must be attentive to you. If you have observed mares and foals, you have noticed the mare nuzzling, bumping, and pushing her baby into obedience. As the foal matures, he learns the limits of his behavior from his dam. Sometimes she has to get pretty rough to get her point across. Once she does, however, the young mule learns to check his behavior with her at regular intervals. For instance, while curiously investigating, he will check the object, then his dam. His attention then returns to the object of his curiosity. It is this kind of attentiveness that you wish to cultivate in your mule. This can be accomplished with a relatively simple procedure. The only tricks in the game are patience and persistence.

First, put your mule into a reasonably small pen, preferably with square corners because this will give you more of an edge. If you are right handed, hold your halter and lead in your left hand and approach the mule from the side, toward the point of his shoulder. Never approach from directly in front or from behind, because he cannot see you clearly and you may frighten him. When he does move away from you, you want him to track to the right if you are right handed. If you are left handed, the situation is reversed. Upon your approach, mentally record the distance between you and your mule when he begins to move away. This is his space, or safety zone. You will use this distance to herd him into a corner and allow him to stop. When he does stop, he will be looking for a route of escape. He may push his head through the fence and lean, or he may just dash back and forth in the corner. Whatever he does, keep your distance and allow him to settle before moving to the next step. If you are in a round pen, a lot more back-and-forth walking (or running) will be required to get him to settle in one spot!

Next, take a step toward his shoulder, holding your left arm (with halter in hand) out so that it discourages him from backing out of the situation. Extend your right hand toward his head and neck. If he does anything other than face you with his head (i.e., backs up kicking, bolts forward, etc.), smack him once on the rump with your halter and lead and say "Face me!" If you can't keep him in the corner and he gets by you, just follow him and set up the same situation again, then repeat the steps.

He will probably get nervous when you smack him. Take a step back and allow him his space; he cannot face you if he is panic-stricken. Continue this procedure until he stands still and turns his head to you. Then, reward him with a reassuring "Good mule!" If he faces you with his head but his rear is still straight to you, lightly touch him a second time with the halter and lead on his hip to encourage him to move over. If he doesn't move, touch him again a little harder until he complies.

Once he has learned to stop and face you, you can move in more closely as described earlier, talking softly and offering rewards. It will

Dena Hodges with the Lucky Three Ranch broodstock.

take a few times before he will allow you to touch him, so be very patient! When he does, stroke him along his neck first, and work your way slowly up to his head. Keep your left arm out enough so that he will not back out of the situation.

Wrap the fingers of your left hand securely around the noseband of the halter, and slip your right arm under and around your mule's neck. Then step to the left side of your mule, just in front of his shoulder. Adjust your arms so that you can grab his nose with your left thumb and slip the noseband over the nose. He will probably try to jerk away, but this position will give you the best leverage. If he does manage to get away, smack him on the rump once more and repeat the entire procedure.

While you are trying to get the halter on, move calmly and quietly, and speak in reassuring tones. Reward him with good strokes and treats if he allows you to halter him. This work in the smaller area does transmit to the larger areas; you have taught him to submit when cornered rather than flee. There may be days when he still makes you chase a little because he needs to maintain some self-esteem, and sometimes he may just be playful. He will not evade you for nearly as long, however, and it will be a lot easier to catch him. Just remember to give a lot of positive reinforcement for compliant behavior!

Lucky Three Selene: First, approach your mule slowly, walking toward the point of his shoulders.

Second, hold the hand with the halter lightly against his behind to discourage any backing up.

Third, when he has settled, bring the halter to his neck, reach around with your right hand, and grab the halter, forming a loop around his neck with your arms.

Fourth, still holding the halter with your left fingers, put your left thumb over his nose to hold him steady, then step around to the other side and fasten the halter. Keep your movements slow and firm so as not to frighten your mule.

And — Success!

Lucky Three Calypso: When introducing your young mule to water for the first time, let him drink from the hose.

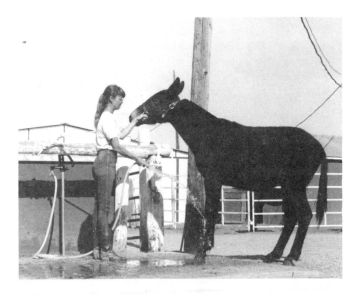

Then drop the hose to his front feet and work your way up his front legs first.

Lucky Three Calpyso: When cleaning the hind feet at first, stand away from the foot. You can slowly begin working your leg under him each new time until you can finally rest his hind leg on your leg.

Once your mule has been handled extensively as a baby, cleaning his feet should pose little problem.

Always remember to reward your mule for his good manners and obedience.

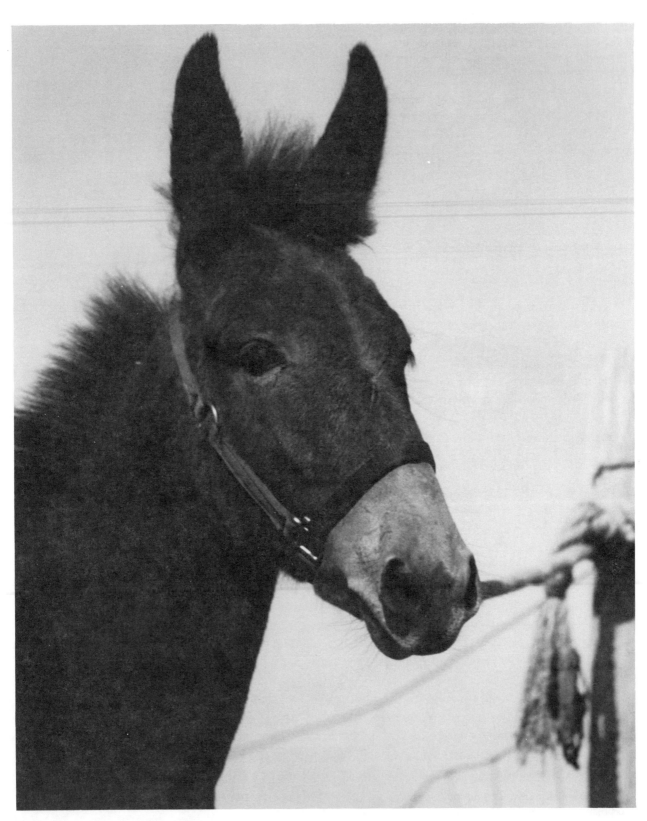

Lucky Three Felicia's Fairytale, 1990.

CHAPTER VII

Teaching Your Mule to Load

You begin to establish a basic disciplinary rapport with your young mule by giving him lots of love and affection and by having relatively low expectations. By the time he is almost a yearling, however, your mule should load easily and should begin to exhibit appropriate ground manners during grooming and trimming sessions. He may not stand quietly while you are away, but he should stand upon your approach. His attention span is still rather short at this stage, however, so be contented with his cooperation at the most important intervals during your sessions. For example, insist that he stand quietly while you hold each foot (praising him lavishly with encouraging words as he complies), but do not expect him to stand perfectly still after you have released each foot. Encourage the quiet behavior, but do not forcefully insist on it until you are ready to go on to the next foot, or to the next step in your routine. By insisting on his attention for only short periods of time, you lessen his chances of failure and frustration. As he matures, his attention span will lengthen, and he will become more willing to comply with your demands.

When your mule is leading confidently in and around disturbing obstacles, it is time to begin teaching him to load into a trailer. By this time, he should be weaned. Foals will generally load with their dams relatively easily, but as a weanling, he will begin to load in accordance with the demands that you place upon him.

Begin by coaxing him into the trailer with gentle words, lots of strokes, and his favorite treats. If he climbs into the trailer easily, reward him lavishly and stay in the trailer for a few minutes before unloading. If he just won't budge, attach a long, stout line to his halter. Run it into the trailer, around a snub, and back out to you. Stand behind and to one side of your mule, holding the line in one hand and the whip in the other. Tap him gently below his hocks and ask him to "Walk." If you have been consistent with this verbal command, he should understand that this means "Go forward." When he steps forward, take up the slack in the line and reward him. Repeat the procedure until he is in the trailer, then reward him accordingly.

If he begins to fight the line, maintain the tension on the line and step aside until he has stopped, then ask him again to go forward. It is very important at this stage not to allow him to back up! A mule learns exactly what you teach him, and if you allow him to back up during loading, it could become a bad habit! When you have a mule that is being difficult, sometimes it is better to use two people, one on the whip and one on the line. If the experience is executed with love and patience, your mule will soon learn to load easily. Remember—consistent repetition is what builds habits, good or bad.

It is often much easier to teach the young mule to load than it is to teach the mule that has had a bad experience with loading. He is not always easily coaxed with goodies and positive reinforcement. Some young mules can also pose a problem. For this reason, you may have to use a slightly modified approach.

It is always best to have two persons while loading for safety purposes, but it isn't absolutely necessary. The first point to remember is to not be rushed during loading. Animals that are already nervous about loading will only become more resistant, and otherwise docile animals can become nervous. Make sure that your animal is tacked up with a stout nylon halter (one that will not break) and a twenty-five-foot lead of the same caliber. A heavy-gauge nylon lunge line works well. When attaching the lead to the halter, do *not* use the snap. Tie the lead directly to the halter ring with a knot that will not slip or come loose, and never use a chain that will cause pain or injury to your animal. It is always best to cover your animal's legs with shipping boots or leg wraps of some sort to protect him from injury during loading or transporting. If your mule is a kicker, also use hock protectors. If he likes to throw his head around, use a poll guard. Sheets or blankets (depending on weather conditions) will help to protect the rest of his body.

Once he is tacked up for transporting, reassure him with a calm and soothing voice, offer him a small tidbit, and lead him quietly to the door of the trailer. Lead him only as close as he is willing to go easily. Then, proceed into the trailer ahead of him, holding the excess lead.

Find a spot where you can take two wraps around a sturdy object, snub your mule, and continue your line out the side of the trailer and back to behind your animal. This is where you will stand during loading. Your lead line will go from the animal, into the trailer, around a snub, and down the outside of your trailer. Then, when your animal moves forward toward the trailer, you can take up the slack easily while encouraging him from behind with a medium-length whip that serves as an extension of your arm.

Most equines need an opportunity to survey the situation before they decide that it is really not all that threatening. If you take a step or two at a time, they will eventually go in with little or no resistance.

If you are loading on the left, make sure that your lead comes out of the trailer on the left side. If you are loading on the right side, your lead should come out the right side of the trailer. This will aid in keeping your animal lined up straight behind the trailer.

When you wish for your mule to load, give a cluck, then give the command "Get up there!" If he takes a step forward, take up your slack and hold tight. Wait for him to settle before you ask him to move again. If he is resistant, encourage him to step forward by tapping him behind his rear fetlocks, one leg at a time. If he still won't go forward, he may try to back up. Do not allow this! Hold your snub firmly and wait until he stops struggling before each tap with the whip. When he discovers that he cannot back up, his attention will refocus forward. If he is a nervous animal, reward him moderately when he ceases to struggle and stands quietly. Do not hurry an animal that is struggling, because this will only make him fight harder and heighten the possibility of injury to yourself and to him. When he has ceased struggling, ask him to go forward again.

An equine's depth perception is different from ours; therefore, give your mule plenty of time to survey the situation, particularly if he has to step up into the trailer. Make sure that he has slack enough to put his nose to the floor at the trailer opening the first couple of tries before you snub him more tightly. This will prevent his legs from sliding under the edge of

Lucky Three Pantera and Ferrara.

the trailer and possibly causing injury. Every time he puts slack into the lead after he has a foot up on the trailer floor, be sure to take it up so that he is snubbed continually. The animal that is allowed to go backward will often use this avoidance behavior if he learns that he can do it, even if he is not fearful. The same applies to animals that are perpetually loaded into trailers with treats. They will eventually take advantage of you and refuse to load easily. A good reward system is essential; however, it must be backed up with a tendency to minimize resistive or avoidance behaviors whenever possible.

When your animal has all four legs securely on the trailer floor and is standing quietly, attach the breech strap behind him and close the doors *before* you release your snub and go to the front to tie him off. You can reach his head through the escape, or feed doors, in most trailers. The open sides of a stock trailer afford easy access. In an enclosed slant-load, you can step in and

tie him easily if the doors are closed behind you and your animal knows that there is no escape. When he is loaded and secured, give him a reassuring word and a treat for a job well done.

As you drive down the road, try to make smooth stops and turns to assure your animal a comfortable and nonthreatening ride. When he learns that he will not be harmed in any way, you will be able to load him more easily each time. Eventually you will be able to fade out your twenty-five-foot lead entirely and send him into the trailer from behind with his lead draped over his back.

When unloading, simply reverse the procedure. At first, let him back out as quickly as he wants to, but maintain your hold on the end of the line so that you can stop him once he is out of the trailer. As he becomes more comfortable with the process, he will back more slowly on his own. If your animal tends to want to explode out the back of the trailer, be sure that he is untied in front before you open the doors to unload him. If he starts fighting the tie rope inside the trailer, he could be severely injured. In addition, you do not want to foster any claustrophobic tendencies with a bad experience. Do not allow your animal to turn around inside the trailer unless he is in hand and at your command! Always insist, at least in the beginning, that he back out. Continually hold his head to achieve this goal. If he gets stuck, you can step into the trailer in front of him, maintain contact on the lead at the halter ring, and push on his chest to encourage him to back out carefully, one step at a time.

If you follow these guidelines carefully and patiently, your loading and unloading nightmares should cease, leaving much more time for fun and enjoyment.

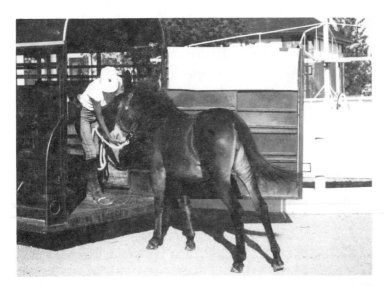

Lucky Three Felicia's Fairytale: Upon approaching the trailer, allow your mule plenty of time to sniff and check out the situation.

Each step of the way, stop, allow him to sniff, then coax him some more.

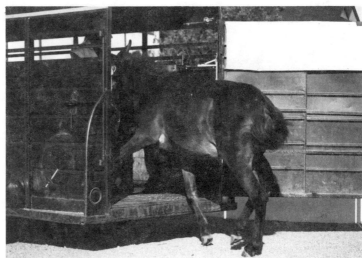

Some youngsters will get to the edge of the trailer and load; other's won't go any farther. If your mule will not be coaxed, go to the procedure outlined on pages 33 and 34.

If your mule can't be coaxed into the trailer, attach a long line to his halter, go through the trailer, then return to you. This will allow you to take up the slack as he approaches the inside of the trailer.

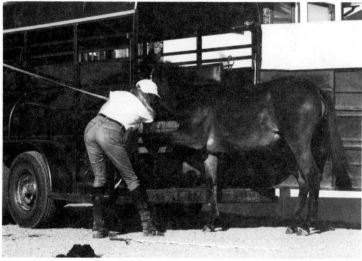

If he is unsure about stepping up into the trailer, help him by putting one foot up on the landing and holding your slack tight so that his next step will be up into the trailer.

A tap of the whip should send him easily into the trailer, after which you should reward him for a job well done.

Gary and Meredith Hodges and Lucky Three Firestorm, National Western Stock Show Halter Champion (48-56 inches).

CHAPTER VIII

Beginning Basic Training

Young mules do not seem to be bothered by the bridle and saddle until they actually begin to work. Often it is best to introduce them to the bridle and saddle at an early age, just as you introduce them to many other obstacles and situations. Because I have so many mules to train at one time, I take this procedure one step further. I bit and saddle the young mules, then put them on a hot walker for thirty to forty-five minutes every other day to accustom them to walking while tacked. If they are thirty months of age or older, I will tie them and mount them before untacking and putting them away.

By the same token, I begin lunging training by asking them to circle around me on the lead rope at various intervals while I am walking around and introducing them to different obstacles. At this time, it is advisable to teach them to begin to walk, to trot, and to halt squarely on the lead.

When practicing halter and showmanship, attach a short chain to your lead rope. Run it through the left side ring on the noseband, underneath the mule's chin, and through the right side ring on the noseband. Then snap it to the ring on the throat latch on the right side. This method keeps the halter balanced and in place on his face when you pull on the lead.

When working the young mule at halter, hold the end of the lead in your left hand and stick your right arm out in front of you. Ask your mule to stay at your right shoulder. As you walk forward, the lead will tighten around your abdomen and put pressure on his face. This is uncomfortable and should cause him to walk forward. Always give the command "Walk on" before you take a step to prepare him to go. If you have been consistent with your verbal commands to this point, he should understand what you mean. Do not look at your mule as you walk on. If you establish eye contact, he will more than likely just stop. When you ask him to "Whoa," you can then turn and look him in the eye and begin to set up his legs so that they are squarely underneath him. If you are consistent with this method, he will know that when your back is turned to him, it is time to move away, and that when you

Lucky Three's Moonrocket, Foxfire, Calypso, and Mister Moon obediently pose for the picture.

turn and face him, he is to stop and square his legs. Over time, this becomes automatic.

Teaching your mule to trot on the line can often start out a little sticky. He may run past you and drag you along somewhat behind, or he may balk and not move at all. If you carry a short whip in your left hand, you can reach behind and tap him if he refuses to move. If he passes you at first, reward him for trotting at all. He will soon discover what you want and will eventually oblige you by staying at your shoulder. Be patient, because this takes much time and practice.

When you ask your mule to turn around, whether it be 180 degrees or 360 degrees, begin by having him take one step forward and then turn. This causes him to set the inside pivot foot and to turn smoothly over his haunches. If you forget to do this, he will be too cramped and will take a step backward, and this will prevent him from setting the pivot foot. If he takes *more* than one step, he will not make the smooth turn over the haunches. Rather, he will take steps in a small circle. Always turn your mule away from you. If he refuses to move around, take your free hand and encourage him by pushing on his shoulder in a push/release

fashion. In the show ring, always turn him so that you are between him and the judge.

Take the time to teach your mule these halter and showmanship techniques, and you will find him a much easier animal to handle while you are on the ground. You can almost eliminate the dangers of him charging past you or running over you if he becomes startled. These techniques also allow him to build more trust and confidence in himself and in you.

Take the time to lead your mule in and around the obstacles that he will encounter as an adult. This will greatly increase his sense of confidence and his trust in you. If he appears to be frightened of an obstacle, simply step up to it yourself, allowing him plenty of slack in your lead line, then talk to him and coax him to it. When he finally takes a step in the right direction, praise him and encourage him until he has approached the obstacle and put his nose to it. This approach will teach your mule to stop and look at an object before deciding that it's too fearful and bolting away. You will be able to coax him up to frightening objects a lot more easily when he is finally going under saddle. Remember—the habits that you build with your mule now will carry into his adulthood.

Lucky Three Melinda's Masterpiece: When leading over for the first time, keep your lead very short in case he decides to pull away. Stay close to his head at first, praise him, and assure him to build confidence. When he is calm about leading over, you can lengthen your rope and allow him to really jump.

Lead your mule through as much "stuff" as you can. Don't move anything out of the way. A little treat at this point may help if he isn't being resistant.

Talk to him; coax him with a soft, reassuring voice.

Lucky Three Moonrocket and Foxfire: Hot walker. We start our young mules out on a hot walker, bitted and saddled. They learn not to be bothered with the equipment and subtly learn the concept of circles. An hour a day also ensures exercise.

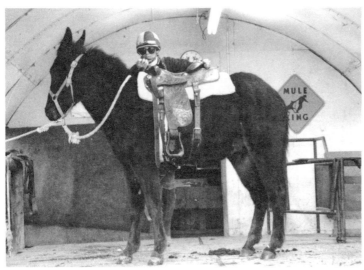

Bitterroot Cody: First mounting Western. As they come off the walker, we begin to get them used to being mounted. Rock your weight in the stirrup on each side.

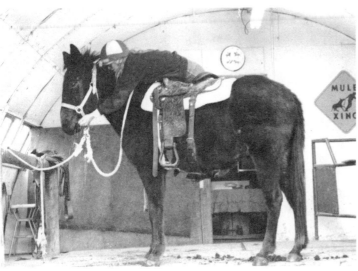

When they are not bothered by the weight shifting, you can lay over their back. Then give them a treat for good behavior and to make them see you.

Lucky Three Calpyso: First mounting English.

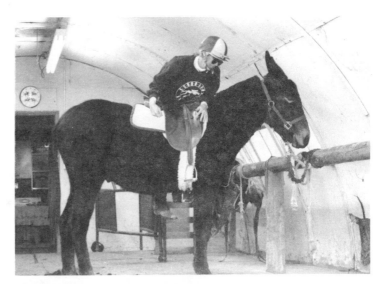

Western or English, the procedure is the same.

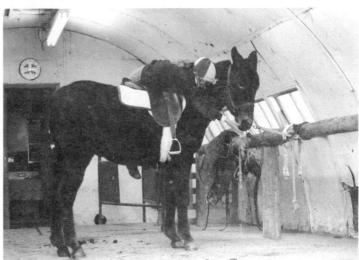

Be sure, however, to do this procedure on both sides!

Lucky Three Melinda's Masterpiece: When teaching the young mule showmanship and correct halter training, hold your lead in your left hand and extend your right arm out in front.

This will teach him to follow your shoulder rather than dragging on the lead rope.

Teaching your mule to trot on the line is done most easily along a fence line. If he gets a little ahead of you, do not worry, just reward him for trotting. He will soon learn to follow your shoulder if he is not jerked back.

Put your arm out in front to encourage your mule to follow your shoulder. Use your right arm to push him off you if he gets too close, or to push him back if he gets too fast.

When setting him up, set the back legs first, then the front while you face the point of his shoulder.

When asking him to turn on his haunches, make sure that you enable him to take one step forward first. Then, you can give little pushes on his shoulder to encourage the turn.

Lunging in side reins at the canter.

CHAPTER IX

Lunging Your Mule

As a two-year-old, your mule should be ready to begin work on the lunge line. The best way to do this is with the help of a round pen, forty to fifty feet in diameter (mine is forty-five feet). The pen should be large enough to allow your mule to canter easily but small enough to allow you to reach him from the center with your lunge whip.

Begin training by allowing your mule to run free with his halter in the pen. The first lesson for him to learn is "Trot on," and the second is "Whoa," but you need to encourage him to expand his vocabulary by calling out the gaits to him as he does them. Position yourself in the center of the pen, then send your mule away to the rail with the command "Trot on." Focus your eyes on his tail and hold the whip out to your side, allowing it to follow well behind your mule. To slow him down, lengthen the distance between his hindquarters and the whip, and move the focus of your eyes farther behind. Allow the mule to travel somewhat freely for awhile (four or five times around the pen) before you ask for the first "Whoa," because he probably has a lot of excess energy to burn! When you are ready, give the command "Whoa," focus your eyes on his, and step sideways and ahead of him. Allow him plenty of space in which to stop. Do not step forward and in front of him, because this movement is too abrupt and will cause him to turn back the other way. When he has halted, walk up to him slowly and praise him with caresses and treats. Stand for a couple of minutes, then repeat the procedure. At this point, insist on the "Whoa" and the direction in which he is to go, but be lenient about the speed of his gait.

When he is responding well to your command to halt, start to regulate his speed. Begin each session by reinforcing the halt; as he goes through the gaits, reinforce them verbally. Begin to become insistent on the upward transitions. Youngsters rarely walk, which is why I begin with the trot to canter. As your mule trots, give the command to canter and move the whip closer to his rear. He should move to canter. Ask him to canter only a few strides at first, then praise him verbally for his compliance. Back off with the whip and allow him to choose his speed again. If he doesn't want

Free lunging Lucky Three Nuggett over two-foot, six-inch oxer.

Lunging at the canter in tack. Round pen should be large enough to facilitate good balance at all three gaits.

to canter, tap him below the hocks with the whip until he does canter.

Next, teach the canter to trot. As your mule canters easily around you, give the command "Trot" and move your whip away from the hindquarters. Take a half-step sideways and ahead of him just long enough to slow him down, then return to your center position. When he trots smoothly, give the command "Whoa" and praise him. Repeat this series of movements as often as necessary to keep your mule slowed to the trot, and praise him verbally for complying. When he responds calmly and easily from canter to trot, move on to the transition from trot to walk, using the same guidelines as just described.

To teach a change of direction, or "Reverse," begin at your mule's most comfortable gait. As he travels around, give the command "Reverse," then turn away from the direction in which he is traveling. Step toward the rail and strike the whip down well ahead of him. *Your* turn should be little more than a half-turn, and the whip should hit the ground almost directly opposite the round pen from your mule. The reason why you should turn around the other way, instead of stepping ahead and in front of him, is to allow your mule to make the distinction between the "Halt" or slow-down and a full reverse. By turning to the new direction, you already are cueing him for what is to come before you must back it up with the whip, allowing him to comply calmly and smoothly.

When he has learned all of his commands well (walk, trot, canter, reverse), snap on the lunge line and review your lessons, excluding the reverse to avoid entanglement. The line itself is a rather small distraction, and your mule should breeze through his lessons. The only addition that you may need to make is giving a short tug on the line for each command to slow down or halt, fading out your own steps until you can stand quietly in the center and give him directions with your voice and through the line.

It is no problem to go from the round pen to an open area if your round-pen work is done correctly and thoroughly. The principle of lunging in an open area is the same whether you are just beginning to lunge or are just finishing your round-pen work. Begin with a shorter line and ask your mule to go around you. As he begins to comply and quits pulling away, gradually lengthen the slack in the line. If you begin lunging with the line, instead of inside the round pen, it could take weeks to get him out and away from you. So don't get impatient!

Work on the lunge can contribute much to your overall well-being and to that of your mule. It is an introduction to training for your mule on a level that he can comprehend, and the communication that you develop with him will establish a good, solid foundation built on mutual love and trust. You are not just teaching your mule *what* to learn, but *how* to learn as well.

Lucky Three Calypso: After hot-walker training, begin free-lunging training. For the initial walking, look down and toward his hindquarters, and point in the direction in which you want him to travel.

To make him speed up, raise your eyes, but keep them fixed on his hindquarters. The faster you want him to go, the more you should look at him directly, and the bigger your body movements should become.

Notice that even at the canter, his ears are waiting for the next command. When free-lunging your mule at the canter, pay close attention to your own body position. Stay behind your mule with your eyes focused on his hindquarters. If he slows down a little, just raise your whip to speed him up. When he is back at the speed that you wish, lower your whip to a horizontal position.

To bring him down from the canter, lower your eyes again and make your movements smaller. When you want him to stop, say, "Whoa." Relax your own body position and wait for him to settle. He will probably look at you first. When he relaxes, you can approach him safely. And don't forget that precious reward for a job well done!

For a right turn-on-the-haunches, the mule tracks to the left, while you make a three-quarter turn to the right and lay down the whip in front of your mule. This causes him to turn back to the right. The whip should land in front of your mule about one-third the diameter of your pen.

A turn to the left is just the opposite. The mule tracks to the right, while you turn to the left and lay down your whip ahead of him. Be sure to give your mule plenty of time and space to execute the turn. After a few good reverses, let him canter on again to relieve any stress.

Lucky Three Calypso: When putting on the bridle, position your right arm between your mule's ears to keep his head down. Hold the bit in your left fingers, and press on the bars of his mouth with your thumb. Push his right ear gently through the crown first, then the left ear.

Check your bit adjustment, then secure the throat latch and other pieces.

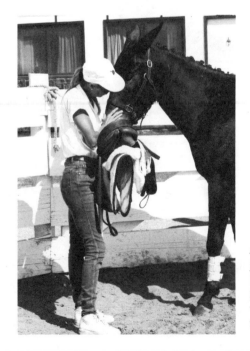

Allow your mule to sniff the saddle, just as you have allowed him to inspect all other strange objects. Stroke his neck and approach him with the saddle. When you push things at a mule, he tends to shy away.

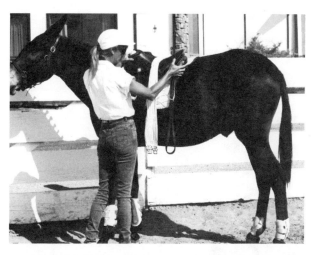

Ease the saddle gently onto his back. Be sure to hold onto any dangling girths or straps. Allow the girth to drop easily onto the other side. Try to keep it from swinging into his legs!

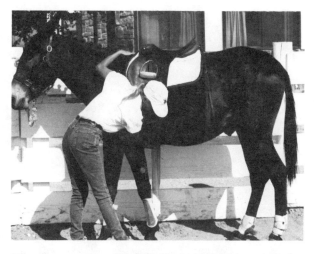

When you reach underneath for the girth, rub your mule gently, yet firmly, along his girth area until you can reach the girth.

Then slowly bring the girth back with your hand and secure it snugly, but not tightly! Take up the slack once more before you go to work.

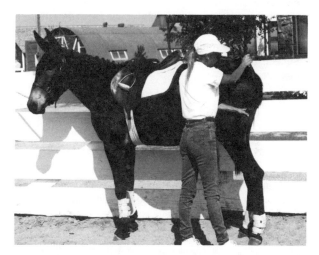

If he tightens his tail when you attach the crupper, you can usually relax him by scratching his rear!

The Elbow Pull

Lucky Three Calypso: The elbow pull encourages your mule to flex his body vertically from head to tail. Adjust it fairly loosely to allow the poll to remain the highest point along the mule's back. The elbow pull applies pressure to four different points on the mule should he resist: at the poll, at the bit, at the elbows (behind the forearm), and across the withers. The beauty of the elbow pull is that, when properly adjusted, it encourages the mule to flex and bend his body, yet the rider does not need to intercede in any way like with draw reins. There is no fumbling with reins and rein adjustments.

Lucky Three Calypso, lunging in the elbow pull. Since he has been bitted and saddled for the hot walker and has learned his commands through free-lunging, you can now review his commands in the elbow-pull rigging to encourage him to arch his back to carry weight.

He may get resistant from time to time with the elbow pull at first, but he will soon learn that if he stays round, there is no interference.

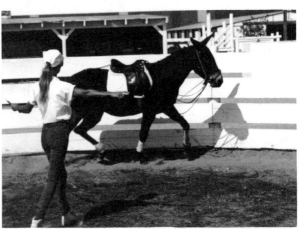

He will then focus his attention back to you and his response will become rounder, smoother, steadier, and more relaxed.

When reversing to the left while he is tracking to the right, make a 360-degree turn to the left and present your whip in front of him about one-fourth the distance of the circle, giving the verbal command to reverse.

When reversing him to the right from tracking to the left, the procedure is just the opposite.

To halt, drop your whip, step just in front of his motion, raise your hands, and give the command to "Halt" or "Whoa."

Lucky Three Calypso: Teach your mule to move away from you on the lunge line, just as you did with the lead rope when he was young. Keep him in close at first, then gradually let out the line and allow him to go to the rail each time.

When he is on the rail, allow some slack in the line. This will encourage him to allow slack in the line when lunging in the open later. When lunging, always be aware of the adjustments needed on your tack and restraints. You want to keep your mule happy and confident!

Work your mule through all of your commands with the lunge line, excluding the reverse. And when he halts nicely and stands quietly, a reward is definitely in order!

Lucky Three Eclipse: Once your mule has achieved a reasonable level of roundness, side reins can help solidify a more uphill balance. Where the elbow pull helped the mule to round by more engagement from the hindquarters, the side reins will strengthen the engagement from the hindquarters while maintaining his roundness.

When lunging in an open area for the first time, begin as you did in the round pen and on the lead with a shorter line. Allow the mule to walk with slack, and only pull if he deviates from the circle. As he pulls less, you can let out your line more.

At the slower gaits, try to stand more still than you did in the round pen; let him take more responsibility for the give-and-take on the line. At faster gaits, walk with him a little to keep the line from tugging on him too abruptly.

As with every exercise, work your mule in both directions to assure even conditioning and response. Keep your eyes focused on his hindquarters, just as you did in the round pen with the whip behind and the line leading forward.

To keep him on the circle at the trot, let the line out with the outside front leg and pull as the outside front leaves the ground to go forward. This will give you the edge without throwing your mule drastically off-balance.

Allow him to become accustomed to the give-and-take of the line before you move on to a faster gait.

PRO PHOTO
Pam Olsen

Lucky Three Nuggett lunging over a three-foot oxer.

CHAPTER X

Ground-Driving in the Round Pen

Once your mule has become proficient on the lunge line, it is time to accustom him to the bit. The most frequently used training bit is the standard broken-mouth snaffle. I must caution you at this point not to use a bit that is too severe on a young mule, because it will create resistance and hamper training. Mules are extremely sensitive to pain and are less likely to comply when they are uncomfortable. If you are gentle and patient with your lessons, your mule usually complies with your wishes at the mere sound of your voice and avoids forcing you to use physical discipline. He basically wants to please. You need only lunge a mule, then a horse, to realize how much quicker the mule is to respond to your voice. A horse may run through the "Halt" for weeks, whereas the mule will learn it almost immediately. It is my belief that the mule will do anything in a snaffle bit if he is taught properly, and if he doesn't, there is no bit severe enough to ensure his compliance.

When you fit the bit for the first time, adjust your headstall more tightly than normal, causing about two wrinkles in the corners of your mule's mouth. It is best not to let him think that he can get his tongue over the bit. Lunge him for a couple of sessions this way. Make sure that the bit is the proper width for his mouth. Then, as his fussing begins to subside, lower the bit in his mouth to the point where one wrinkle at the corners of his lips is barely visible. Lunge him this way until he is comfortable and relaxed with the bit.

Next, introduce a surcingle that fits snugly around your mule's girth. If you do not plan on driving your mule, use a small, light saddle during this stage of training, preferably a pony saddle. You can strap the surcingle around the saddle. Whether introducing the surcingle or the saddle, make your movements slow and deliberate, reassuring your mule with kind words and caresses over his neck, back, and girth. Before bringing the girth around his middle, be sure to rub the area thoroughly to prepare him for what is to come. Cinch up slowly until the surcingle is snug, but not too tight! Again, lunge him in this rigging until he is quiet and relaxed about it. If your mule becomes alarmed and starts to buck, or to carry on in an undesirable

59

fashion, stop what you are doing and calm him. He is not deliberately misbehaving; therefore, do not try to stop him by punishing him. His mind is just locking up from an overload, and what he needs is your praise and reassurance so that he can regain his confidence. Right here is where you have the opportunity to teach your mule to trust you when he is frightened or confused. This will determine whether he will stay with you or flee stressful situations in the future. Review all free lunge exercises with rigging.

At this stage in your mule's training, it is easy to get excited and want to get to the business of riding your young mule. It is easy to forget the stage of ground-driving or to set it aside for driving mules only. Yet, ground-driving is an essential part of the complete training process, especially with mules. Ground-driving teaches the mule all of the fundamentals of riding without the undue stress of the rider. It gives him more time to learn each new lesson and builds his confidence in you and in himself. It sets the stage for a resistance-free learning process. Ground-driving also separates good driving mules from the rest.

Before you actually attach the reins to the bit and begin your lessons, be sure that your mule is relaxed and going comfortably. Like so many humans, mules are not born with good posture; it is something that must be learned and practiced if it is to become habit. Yet, in order for your mule to be truly comfortable and relaxed, good posture is essential. The mule must be taught to round his back and to travel in a balanced manner. To do this, I attach a rigging called an elbow-pull, which is nothing more than a twelve-foot rope with a snap on each end. First, fold your rope in half and drop it over your mule's poll. Take the "reins" on each side and run them through the snaffle rings toward his chin, then down between his front legs and up to his back. Adjust the tension on the rope so that the mule's poll is even, or slightly higher than, his withers, and snap the rope to your surcingle on each side. If your elbow-pull rope is long, you may snap it to itself over your mule's back. (At this point, I must caution against securing these snaps on a horse, because a horse might rear and go over backward. With

a horse, use a loosely tied lariat.) If the mule now tries to raise his head too high, the elbow-pull puts pressure on the poll, on the mouth, on the elbows, and on the back. When he travels in frame, there will be no pressure. The beauty of the elbow-pull is that it allows the mule to regulate his own posture, discouraging resistance. Lunge him in the elbow-pull until he has it figured out. His gaits will smooth out before your very eyes, and his responses through transitions will become more easy and fluid. When he responds easily to all of your commands in the elbow-pull, it is time to snap on your driving lines.

Leave the elbow-pull in place, snap on your drive lines, and run them through the rings on your surcingle (or, tie your stirrups together underneath and run the lines through them). Stand in the center, as you have done before, and work your mule around you. Accustom him to pressure on the bit slowly and easily in conjunction with appropriate commands. Now that you have two reins, you can reintroduce the "Reverse" without getting tangled in the lines. Simply give the command "Reverse," pull gently on the outside rein, and loosen your inside rein, causing your mule to turn into the fence and reverse. Spend plenty of time reviewing the basics while you are in the center before you try to actually move in behind your mule. You can slowly start edging your way in behind him when he becomes more accustomed to the drive lines. If he bolts forward and pulls on the lines, go back to the center and try again. If you do not try to get in behind him too fast, he probably won't even worry about you. It may take a week or two to get in behind, so take your time! Not only are you teaching your mule about control, but about trust and companionship as well. The more trusting he is of humans, the more dependable he will turn out to be as an adult.

Once you have worked your way in behind your mule in the round pen, you need to teach your mule to walk forward freely. At this stage, leave the elbow-pull in place to allow your mule to regulate his own posture. Your only concern should be to keep your mule calm and quietly compliant with your commands. At first, your mule will probably be a little "goosey" about having you in behind him, and his speed will vacillate between fast and slow. Talk to him in a low, soothing voice, and praise him when he walks quietly and without fear. Reassure him that this is indeed what you require.

Once he has accepted your position and walks quietly forward, ask him for the "Halt." If he spooks and runs off, stand quietly and wait for him to stop. When he does, reward him for stopping. *Do not punish him for running off.* After all, you have been asking him to go forward; how can you expect him to know the difference between going forward and running off, especially in a round pen? It is far more important to reward your mule for his positive behavior than to give credence to his mistakes! This will lessen the chances of your mule misunderstanding your intentions, and when he does become fearful, he will come to you for assurance.

When he accepts the "Halt,'" you are ready for working on the turn. First, ask him to halt, then give a gentle pull on the rein in the direction of the fence. As you shorten your turning (or direct) rein, let the opposite rein out a little, but maintain contact with the bit. When your mule is again parallel to the fence, release the bit pressure and allow him to walk forward. Timing is everything at this point! The bit release is his reward for completing a successful turn. It is a passive reward that will soon take the place of your frequent verbal and physical rewards as he matures. It is important to practice and improve your own coordination skills at this point in training so that the bit release occurs immediately following your mule's compliance. In this way it is truly a reward. If you are meticulous about releasing the bit immediately after your mule halts, he will always stand quietly on a loose rein.

When your mule is confident about responding to bit pressure on the halts and turns, and when he stands quietly, it is time to introduce the "Back." Ask him to halt as you would for the turn, only this time, pull the rein on the side away from the fence first. Pull this rein until he moves the corresponding front foot back one step, then pull the rein on the other side until his other foot comes back. Then reward him for two steps back. Remember—when the foot

moves back, you must release pressure on the bit slightly to give the passive reward for his compliance. As he begins to understand what you are asking, you will be able to ask for more and more steps backward.

If you have a spirited mule or one that is easily distracted, you may have to approach the "Back" a little differently. Drive him straight to the fence and halt, then ask for a step back from each front foot. Be sure to keep contact on both reins while tightening the one rein or you might get a "Turn" instead of a "Back." Once he has stepped back on each front foot, allow him to go forward again to the fence. Let him turn and proceed down the rail before you try to halt him again. Reward him for the backup with your voice and by releasing the bit. Asking him to halt, back, then halt again will only aggravate him and will probably produce confusion and resistance. Young mules simply don't like to stand still too long (like young children). This problem usually works itself out over time if you are patient and understanding. Do not ask a young mule to halt any longer than necessary.

Mules are like people in that certain individuals learn more quickly than others. Still, there is more to training than just learning "the moves." The time that you spend in the round pen will determine how trustworthy and dependable your mule will be as an adult. If you are meticulous about your training (executing cues calmly and deliberately, reassuring bad behavior, and reinforcing good behavior), your mule will soon come to realize that you are the source of his pleasure, and he will look forward to his sessions with you. If you are punitive, he will probably prefer the company of anyone else but you! The happy mule actually prefers to be with humans rather than with other mules, and he will meet you with a willingness to please that is unmatched. Take your time and learn all you can in the round pen before you go on to the next steps in training. Establish a good rapport with your mule, perfect your own cues and commands, and always try to facilitate willing compliance in your mule. The speed and fluidity of his responses will all come in good time.

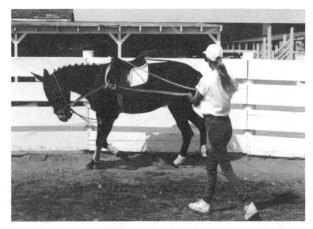

Begin long-line driving from the middle as you did when you were lunging him.

Quietly begin to step in closer behind him. Take as long as necessary for him to feel comfortable.

When turning, give the verbal command to "Haw" or "Gee," then pull the rein straight back toward your hip.

Be sure to give him plenty of release for the turn.

When he has sufficiently turned, give the command to "Walk on."

Lucky Three Foxfire: When using the crupper for the first time, do not be alarmed when your mule objects. Allow him time to get used to it before going to work. Soothe him with your voice until he is no longer tense.

Draw Reins

Lucky Three Mae Bea C.T.: The main strength of the mule lies in his head and neck. If he is allowed to raise his head and open his jaw, there is no way to stop him. The use of draw reins in this manner (shown in the photo) will not allow him to lift his head and neck, and the cavesson (securely tight) will not allow him to open his jaw. You are, with this method, just taking your reins right through the snaffle rings and fastening them at the girth, between the front legs, giving yourself a lot more leverage at the bit itself. If your mule "muscles" his way through this rigging, he really means he doesn't want to comply, and you'd better not drive him!

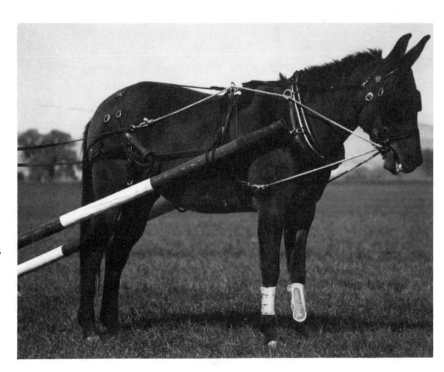

Cindy Powell and Lucky Three Stardust compete in trail class in a mule show on the East Coast.

CHAPTER XI

Ground-Driving in the Open

Ground-driving in a small corral, or round pen, is beneficial to the young mule in many ways. In addition to receiving basic training in acceptance of the bit and rein control, he learns to confide and trust you, his trainer. Conversely, you are able to assess and understand the personality of each individual mule with which you work. The second stage of ground-driving will enable you to decide the type of equine athletics for which your mule is best suited.

When he complies easily to your commands to walk, trot, back, and turn, it is time to move on to the next stage of ground-driving. Review all previous lessons, then introduce your mule to a much larger area where you can begin to work as you did in the round pen. A mule can become nervous and frightened when faced with this larger area, or he can become more playful. The larger area may remind him of his days romping in an open field, and in his own mind, this may seem perfectly alright. Obviously, it is not alright!

If your mule forgets his lessons and bolts away from you, you need to make some tack adjustments to give yourself more leverage. For the high-headed mule, attach a set of reins in a draw-rein fashion, fastening the lines between the front legs at the girth, through the snaffle rings, and back to you. For the mule with a normal head carriage, fasten the lines to the girth just behind the forearms outside the front legs, through the snaffle rings, and back to you. As long as your mule complies with your wishes, be kind with your hands and don't hold him too tightly in frame as he goes forward. If he does try to pull away, the draw-reins should give you enough leverage to stop him.

At this point, you can decide if this mule will be suitable for driving. If he pulls against you continually or manages to run off, he is a risky driving prospect. If he continues to learn his commands and movements in the open area with minimal fussing, he is a good candidate for driving, exhibiting good sense and valuable trust of his trainer. Even if I have a difficult mule, I still try to finish this stage of training with him. I simply lower my expectations of him and do not hitch him to a vehicle at a later time.

Whether driven or ridden, a young mule is faced with a world full of potential "killers!"—objects that frighten him to no end. The more you can introduce at this phase of ground-driving, the calmer and safer your mule will be later. When he is responding well to his basic commands at this stage, begin adding obstacles to your driving area. Start by placing cones strategically to enable you to begin ground-driving patterns, including serpentines, figure-eights, and circles of all sizes. Begin with larger circles, then decrease their size gradually. When these patterns become relatively controlled, add some variety to the routine by throwing out walk-over logs, a bridge, a mailbox (to stop at), or a straight back-through. Use your imagination to help him become accustomed to various kinds of "spooks;" drape things on the area fence and ask him to proceed quietly by these objects. If he is fearful in the beginning, don't hesitate to lead him to the objects first and reassure him that everything is alright. Stand at the obstacle for as long as it takes for him to become quiet, then go back and try to drive him on by.

During this phase of training, I introduce the whip for lateral control. For instance, if the mule is shying from a jacket (or other object on the fence), I lead him to it and allow him to check it out thoroughly while I praise him for being so bold. Then I attempt to drive him by it. His first inclination is to hesitate, then comply, but he probably would swing in his haunches in an attempt to face the obstacle again. At this point, I gently tap his hip, holding the reins straight, and urge him to continue forward. If the obstacle is to his right, his haunches will swing to the left; therefore, I tap the left hip, causing him to move away from the pressure of the whip and back toward the rail. Be sure that you do not restrict his forward motion as you tap him, because he must have somewhere to go! Now reverse and drive by your obstacle the other way, introducing the whip and the obstacle to both sides of your mule's body. He may be compliant going one way, but the other way may be a whole new story! Doing a maneuver on both sides produces an animal that is balanced in mind and body.

Ground-driving through numerous trail obstacles and patterns can give your mule much stability, making his eventual experience under saddle much easier with a lot less resistance. Through this process, he strengthens his trust in you, he increases his own confidence, and he lengthens his overall attention span. Exposure to many different situations lessens his fear and increases his ability to cope with the hustle and bustle of the world around him.

Keep your trail obstacles relatively straight and simple at this stage. You can use any number of items: logs, cavalletti, things draped on a fence, tarps on the ground, and even water obstacles. When he has become proficient at these types of obstacles, only then can you move on to obstacles that require more lateral control.

You can begin to assess your mule's strong points throughout this stage of training. If he handles the obstacles easily and calmly, he will probably be a good prospect for driving, trail, and pleasure. If he is a bit nervous but compliant, he might be a better prospect for more high-energy athletics such as reining, gymkhana, or jumping. Watch how he moves through the obstacles. Pay attention to his attitude, the way in which he picks up his feet, his length of stride, and his ability to balance himself, because they will indicate his future forte. There is a lot more to ground-driving than meets the eye. Take the time not only to teach your mule, but to teach yourself about him. If you do, the career that you choose can be pursued happily and will be more likely to generate success!

Lucky Three Nuggett: Ground-driving teaches your mule the relationship of your verbal commands to hand-rein cues. When ground-driving, be sure to carry any excess line in your hands so that you don't trip or get tangled in it. You can ground-drive as many different patterns as you can ride. Concentrate on keeping your mule calm, supple, and soft in the mouth.

When driving, adjust your reins so that you have a good feel of his mouth, and try to walk along in unison with your mule's hind legs. Maintain a squeeze-and-release action of the reins for stops, turns, and bending. Steady pressure will most likely cause a runaway. Do lots of circles and bending exercises to achieve lateral suppleness.

Trot the same patterns that you did at the walk. If your mule starts to take off with you, just change your steps so that they work opposite the hind legs to maintain the give-and-take on the reins yet give some resistance to cause him to slow. Ground-driving can be done in restraints or without them, depending on the needs of your individual mule.

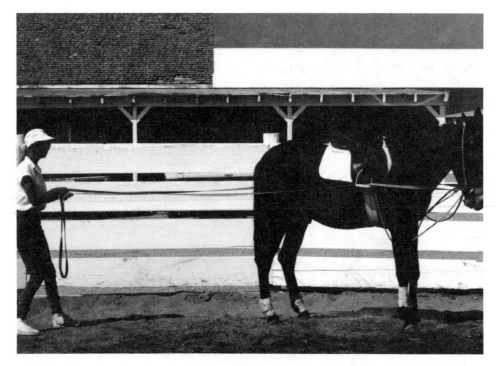

Lucky Three Calypso: Before beginning to back up, alternate your rein pressure to cause your mule to drop his nose and give to the bit. Make sure that your lines are even before starting to back up.

As you back up, squeeze first one rein and then the other. Step backward yourself in unison with the front legs. Do not try to go too fast. Give your mule plenty of time to respond, and keep your hands light.

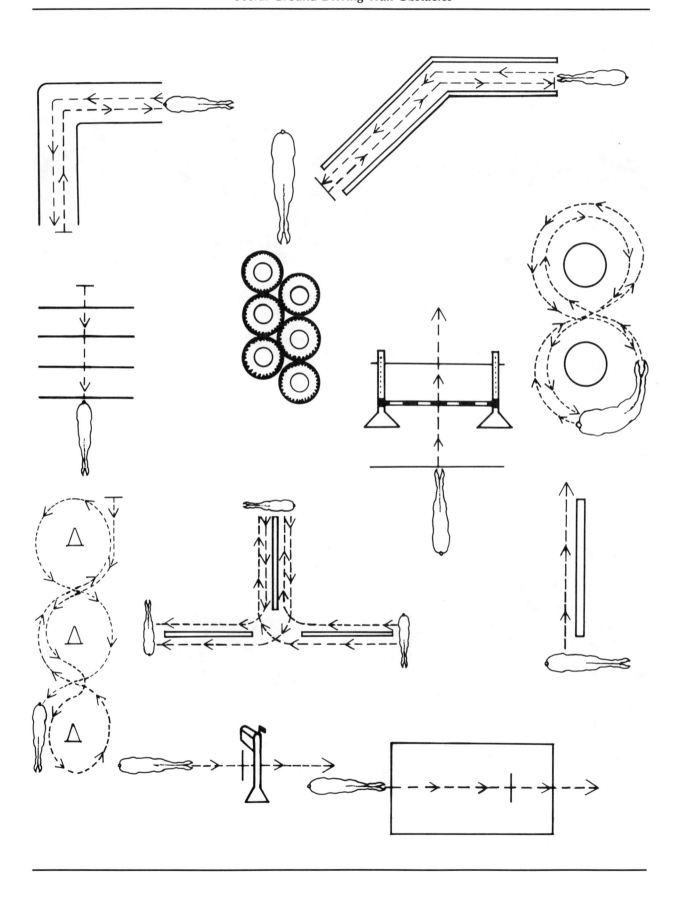

Ground poles can teach many important lessons. The mule learns to look where he is going and to place his feet carefully and deliberately. He also learns the corresponding rein cues to this purpose. Again, you should squeeze and release rein pressure with the hind legs. Remember that you need to space your legs differently for the trot than for the walk. The mule needs more space between the ground poles to accommodate his lengthened stride.

Tires are another obstacle that can be rearranged to accommodate different exercises. You can walk through one or through many. They can be stood on end or flat. You can drive through or ask the mule to do a turn-on-the-forehand with his front legs in the center of the tire.

Learning to stand is just as important as going forward, turning, and backing. The mailbox affords standing practice with a purpose. Be sure to stop long enough to allow your mule to settle.

If you approach an obstacle that causes your mule to shy, just walk to his head and lead him through first. Talk to him calmly and reassuringly.

Once he has been allowed to survey the situation, you should be able to drive him through the obstacle with little problem.

By putting rein pressure on every step, you can control every step that your mule takes. To vary this exercise, try stopping your mule halfway, then proceed.

Drive over as many obstacles as you can think of. The more different exercises you do, the calmer your mule will be under saddle. Take the time to introduce him to the obstacles that seem to frighten him.

When teaching your mule to side-pass a rail, it is best to start with a fence in front of him to keep him from going forward. This will make lateral control much easier.

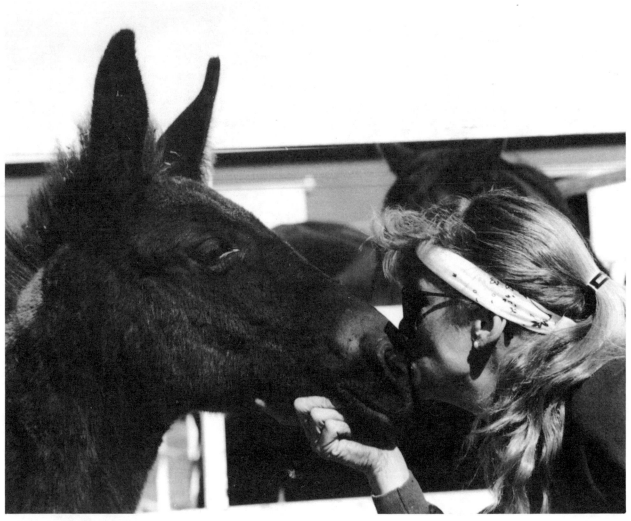

Lucky Three Midnight Victory is big on kisses!

CHAPTER XII

Lateral Work on the Long Lines

It is time to introduce lateral exercises when your mule has become proficient at driving forward and in and around obstacles, and when he backs easily. Introducing lateral movements before he is put into shafts will help him feel less anxious about the confinement of the shafts. He will learn to move his entire body to the side when asked, a maneuver that will allow him to avoid doubling in the middle and thus prevent a wreck in the shafts. He will become accustomed to touch on his sides through the whip cues, desensitizing the areas where the shafts will rest. Lateral exercises teach the mule more than just directional changes through the reins. He learns to balance in the half-halt (a brief squeeze/release action on the reins), to maintain his balance through all the gaits, and to flex his body from head to tail through corners and circles.

The first exercise is to track left at the perimeter fence, then go down the long side and across the short side. Cross the diagonal, then continue across the next short side. Do the same maneuver to the right. As you approach the corner to cross the diagonal to the left, ask your mule to "Haw" for the turn, then ask for a halt when his shoulders and head face the far corner. Hold the reins steady and ask him to move his hindquarters one-quarter turn to the left by tapping him gently on the right side with the whip. If he doesn't understand, squeeze your right rein and allow his head to come to the right a little. This should help swing his haunches to the left. When he has complied, stop and reward him.

Now, allow him to walk forward, and as he does so, lead him to the corner with the left rein, squeezing and releasing pressure with every stride. As you squeeze the left rein, tap his right side with the whip. Keep the right rein steady. Your mule's head should be held straight in front, or it should be cocked only slightly to the right. Repeat this exercise in each direction several times.

It will not take your mule long to figure out what you are asking, but you must be careful about coordinating your cues so that they are clear and concise. You should be squeezing the lead rein and tapping your mule with the whip as the foreleg on the whip side comes forward. Interfering with the forward motion this way causes his stride to move laterally. Each time you make the corner on the diagonal, give the command to "Haw" (left), or "Gee" (right) to solidify these terms in his mind. Be sure that he halts and does his quarter turn on the forehand to get his body parallel to the wall before proceeding forward on the diagonal. If this is not done, he may become anxious or concerned and may run off!

Once he is moving easily across the long diagonal laterally, begin to shorten the distance and increase the angle of lateral movement. Instead of going from corner to corner, go from the corner to the middle of the long side of the arena. Shorten the distance travelled and increase the lateral angle so that your mule will process the lateral movement more clearly in his own mind. This will make him more responsive to half-halts through the reins. Remember—as you cross your diagonals, your mule should be parallel to the wall on the long side! When you first try the short diagonal, allow your mule to walk straight down the remainder of the long side, down the short side, and around the corner to take the next short diagonal in the same fashion, only in the opposite direction. When he understands this, you can begin to vary your pattern.

Next, cross the short diagonal as you did before, only make a small circle as you reach the middle of the wall on the long side. Direct your mule's shoulders to the next short diagonal, halt, and move his hindquarters over a quarter turn. Complete another short diagonal in the opposite direction. Allow him to walk through the corner, down the short side of the arena to the next corner, then repeat the pattern. In essence, you will be making a "<" from the first corner, to the middle of the opposite wall, then back to the next corner on the same side where you began. If your mule has trouble going all the way from corner to wall, ask him to go only to the center of the arena, then back to the next corner. Whichever way you begin, be sure to circle, halt, and quarter-turn before you ask for the new diagonal each time.

Continue to vary your patterns, to shorten the distance of the diagonals, and to increase the angles. Place solid obstacles strategically along the wall and ask your mule to move away from the wall, around the obstacles, then back to the wall. Put some cones in a row and move him through them using a lateral, rather than straight-forward, motion.

When your mule understands these basics of lateral motion, you can teach him to side-pass on the long lines. Have him face the wall while you stand in behind. If you wish him to move to the left, keep your right rein connected and steady while you simultaneously squeeze/release the left rein and tap him gently with the whip on the right side. To go right, do just the reverse. If you take this slowly, step-by-step, stride-for-stride, your mule will soon learn what is being asked. In the beginning, take the time to praise him for each correct step.

When he side-passes well, teach him to wheel around. Stand with your back to the wall. Using the same cues as for the side-pass, ask him to move over until he reaches the wall. Use your verbal commands—"Haw over" or "Gee over"—to aid him. When he succeeds, praise him lavishly. Then ask him to wheel over the other way to the wall on your other side. Verbal cues are extremely important at this stage, because your hands and body are not as accurate as you would like to believe and may cause the mule some concern. The verbal cues reinforce what is being asked.

Probably the most important thing that you can do for your mule at this stage of training is to coordinate your hand and whip cues so that they are consistent and nonpunitive. Avoid pulling on the reins. Hold your reins gently but firmly in both hands, with your thumbs up at all times. When you give a rein cue, go from a gentle, firm hand to an actual hard squeeze, then release back to the firm, gentle hand. Big movements produce big results. Therefore, do not allow your reins to go slack before you cue your mule for a new direction, or he may just turn around! By the same token, do not tap him too hard with the whip, or he may do a lot more than just move over! Practice holding the whip and the reins so that your movements are smooth and controlled. This will facilitate a better understanding between you and your mule.

The ground work for a well-turned driving or riding mule is laid with beginning work on the long lines. Bea and Ciji ground-driving with Meredith Hodges for pleasure.

Gail Altieri and Ole King Jole quietly negotiate the poles in a classic trail class.

If you do all of these exercises correctly, you will soon be able to drive your mule around and through any kind of trail obstacles with him remaining calm and compliant. Take the time to let your mule learn rein and pressure cues on the long lines, and you will greatly simplify the actual breaking process, whether he is to be hitched to a vehicle or saddled. It is really only logical to allow him to finish kindergarten before moving on to grammar school. After all, most kids learn their ABCs before they are required to form words and sentences. Try to give your mule the same consideration.

Lucky Three Nuggett: Doing this exercise along the rail in the beginning helps your mule to stay more lateral and less forward. As he begins to understand, try to keep him lighter and lighter in the mouth. Don't be alarmed if this exercise is very awkward in the beginning. It will take you and your mule a little time to get into sync with each other, and this is what learning is all about. Although you are checking and releasing the front legs with your reins, you should still be walking in unison with the mule's hind legs to perpetuate the forward motion.

Actually, these exercises can be done without the whip to start if your cueing is relatively coordinated. You soon will find that your mule will perform at the slightest touch of the reins. The angle of the lateral motion will be determined by your own body position. Do this exercise from a very small angle to the completed side pass. When he is light and supple and easily responsive, you can move into the open and begin the foundation for the leg yield.

A mule tends to lean into pressure, which means that you should begin to drive him laterally by guiding him in the direction you wish him to go, rather than driving from the other side and pushing him in that direction. Once he understands, you can go to the pushing position. When driving him in the open, make your movements as light and smooth as possible. Take it one step at a time, and be rewarding. Looping the rein on the off side from you around his haunches will help you to keep his leg-yield straight and parallel to the rail.

To reverse the direction of your lateral movement, simply change sides of your mule and guide him to the new direction. Always work toward lightness, suppleness, and flexibility in your own hands to bring this out in your mule. Soon your mule will become supple and light when driven laterally in the open.

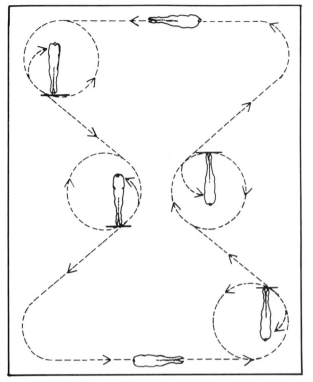

A: Crossing the long diagonal.

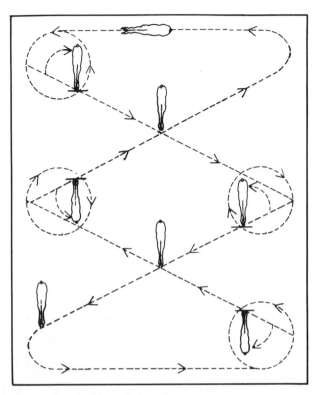

B: Crossing the short diagonal.

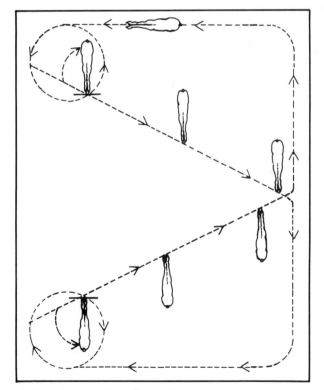

C: Crossing two short diagonals.

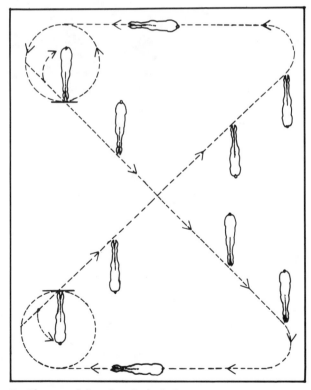

D: Change of direction through the center.

Meredith Hodges ground-driving a ranch team, Lucky Three Ciji and Lucky Three Mae Bea C.T.

CHAPTER XIII

Adjusting Your Harness

Before harness training, make sure that you have a properly fitting set of harness. If your mule is uncomfortable in any way, he could develop sores or raw spots on his body. And if he is uncomfortable, he may become resistant in his performance. Check the harness to make sure that it is in good repair. Harness that is too old, dry, or cracked can break and cause a number of undesirable results. If the tugs break anywhere, your mule can become detached from the cart and run off. If the breeching pieces break, the cart can run up on his rear and cause him to bolt. Each part of your harness plays an important role in the overall balance and performance of your vehicle. If one piece is loose or broken, it will offset the balance of the entire rigging and will most likely cause an accident. So check your harness carefully before using it.

To harness your mule, place the surcingle and breeching on him first. Adjust the surcingle snugly, but not too tightly. Check it at intervals to make sure that your mule has not expanded or that it has not become too loose. Also, fit the breeching and crupper snugly, but not tightly. Add your collar and hames (or breast collar if you have that type of harness). You should be able to fit the fingers of your hand under the collar in front, and the collar should ride just in front of the shoulders. The breast-collar type needs to be adjusted so that it is high enough in front so as not to interfere with the movement of the shoulders.

Put on your bridle and attach the reins last. When you hitch your mule to the vehicle, the tugs, the breeching, and the surcingle should all be attached snugly to assure proper response of the vehicle to the mule. When the mule takes his step forward, the vehicle should move *with* him, not a second later. When he backs up, the first step should also move the vehicle. If there is any slack in your harness, the movement will become abrupt. This could startle your mule and cause problems.

Take the time to check everything before you start. Once a mule has become frightened of driving for any reason, it is very difficult to get him to relax and accept it again. Better to be safe than sorry!

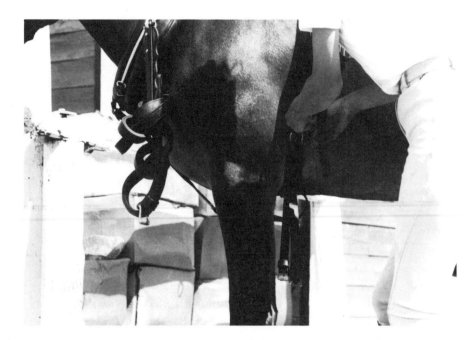

Lucky Three Mae Bea C.T. and Ciji: Be sure to check all straps for cracking or breakage.

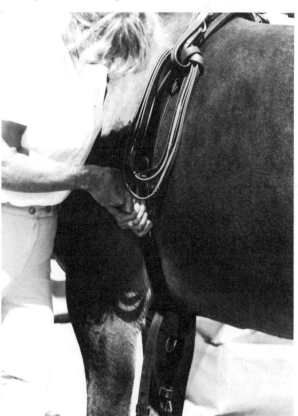

Place the surcingle and breeching over your mule's back, and tighten the surcingle first.

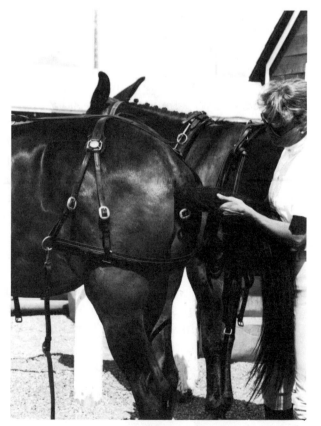

Then go to the tail and smooth the top hairs before bringing the crupper around it.

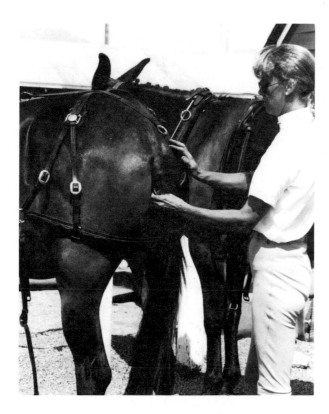

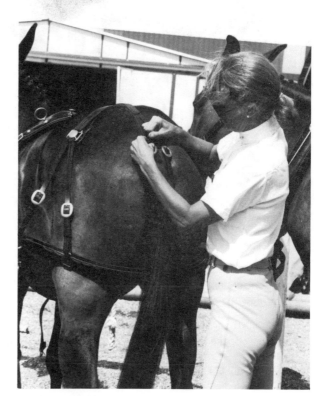

Above, left: Stroke your mule as you bring the crupper under the tail to encourage him to relax.

Above, right: Fasten the crupper on the other side of the tail in a snug position.

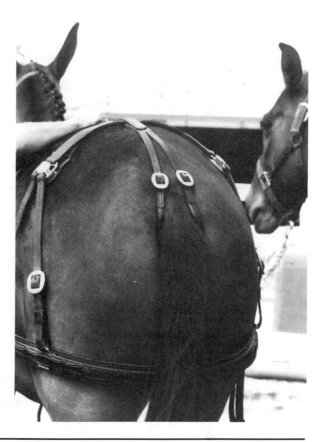

Right: The tailpiece of the harness should come off of the surcingle smoothly and snugly, but not tightly.

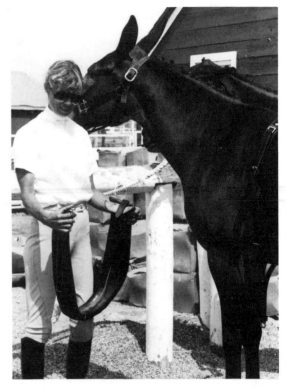

Above: The surcingle and breeching in place.
Right: Collars today come apart at the top.

Below, left: Loop the collar around his neck and fasten the buckle at the top.
Below, right: Buckle the false martingale to keep your collar in place and immediately attach the other end to the surcingle.

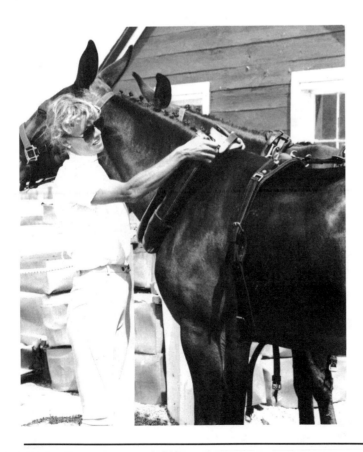

Check your buckles and straps to make sure that they are all lying flat and straight.

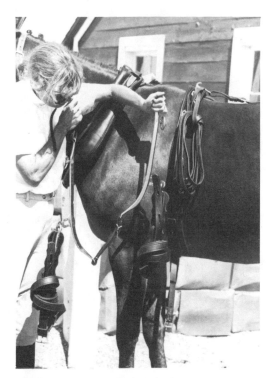

The hames are attached at the bottom.

Loop them round the collar and fasten at the top.

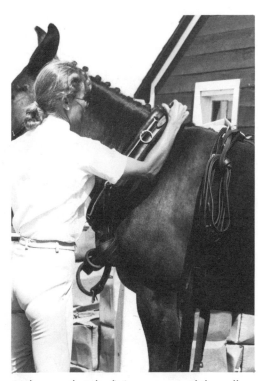

Make sure that the fit is snug around the collar.

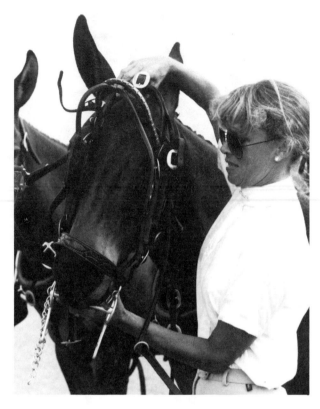

Above, left: You should be able to fit your hand down the front of the collar, and it should rest into the groove of his shoulder so as not to rub or cause injury.

Above, right: Bring the bridle over his head as shown.

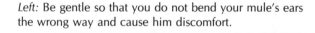

Left: Be gentle so that you do not bend your mule's ears the wrong way and cause him discomfort.

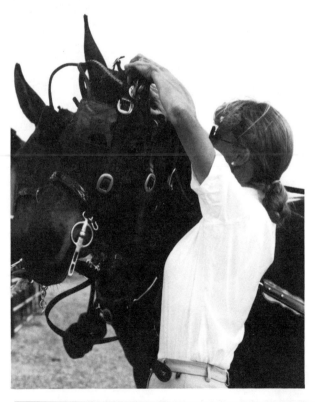

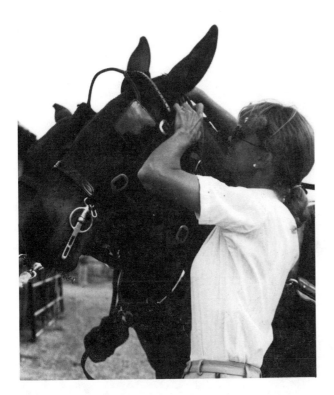

Check your bridle to make sure that all connections are in good repair and that your bridle fits well.

Adjust your curb chain so that you can get two fingers in underneath it.

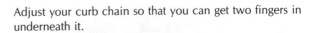

When you begin to ground-drive your team, keep your ties between them reasonably loose. It is easiest to drive with one set of reins controlling both mules at once, with the right rein guiding both mules to the right and the left rein guiding both mules to the left.

Meredith Hodges enjoys ground-driving in the open fields with Lucky Three Ciji and Lucky Three Mae Bea C.T.

CHAPTER XIV

Finishing the Driving Mule

When your mule is performing all of the exercises successfully, it is time to decide if he is to go into harness or onto the saddle-breaking process. Each mule and trainer will make this decision. Those of you who wish to drive your mules should definitely recruit some help at this stage of training to assure the safety of yourself and of your mule!

Always begin your lessons by reviewing all that he has learned. When he is warmed up and quietly complacent, introduce him to the shafts. Have your assistant hold the mule with a lead rope while you attach two long poles to each side of your mule's body. Behind him, make sure that the poles are tied together somehow so that they cannot spread too far apart. When they are in place, begin to drive your mule around as you did in the beginning throughout his "Forward" exercises. Your assistant should walk along with you, holding the lead line but not interfering with your rein cues. If your mule becomes alarmed, just stop and comfort him with praise and caresses, then move on again. You may only be able to take two or three steps with the shafts the first time, or they may not bother him at all; each mule is different. At any rate, take as much time as you need, and exercise as much patience as you can to help him overcome his fear. This stage should go quickly.

When he is totally quiet about the shafts, think about hitching him up. First, have your assistant walk your breaking cart around while you and the mule follow closely behind. This will allow your mule to see what the cart does and hear how it sounds over bumps and such. Gradually work him up to walking on both sides of the cart to establish a new perspective. The more ways he can perceive the cart before you harness him to it, the calmer he is likely to be.

Before harnessing, check all of your equipment for weak spots and fit, and be sure to equip yourself with a helmet or hard hat. Most breaking carts do not have brakes; I recommend that you have them installed. Creating a drag on the cart sometimes can prevent a serious runaway, or at least slow it down.

The first time that you hitch your mule to the cart, let him become accustomed to the confinement without actually going anywhere. Have your mule tied securely in a place where he will not be injured should he decide to flail his body around. Have your assistant stand at the mule's head to keep him quiet while you hitch the mule to the cart. Tie the mule securely with both a halter and lead over his bridle. When he is hitched to the cart, walk around him, touching his body with a comforting hand while you shake and rattle everything you can. If he becomes nervous and unsettled, stop for a minute, pet him, then keep it up again until he is quiet. When it bothers him no more, reward him and put him away. Do not try to drive him anywhere until he is content to stand quietly. If he doesn't seem bothered about the shaking and rattling of the cart and harness, you can lengthen the lead with which he is tied so that you can back him up a few steps without untying him. This will allow the mule to feel the cart move with him, yet he will be unable to go anywhere if he becomes frightened. Do not go beyond this lesson the first day.

When your mule is quiet with the cart at the hitch rail, it is time to trust him a little. Have your assistant help you review your previous lessons, then release your mule from the wall. Your assistant can aid your control with a lunge line at your mule's head while you walk behind the cart and drive the mule in a small circle. Again, make sure that your assistant's lead is attached to a halter and not to the bridle. Otherwise, the lead may interfere with reins. As your mule quiets down, have your assistant gradually let out the slack on the lunge line and allow the mule to circle around him. Increase the diameter of the circle as the mule is able to cope with it. Begin work on the walk and eventually increase it to the trot. Do not make these first hitched lessons too long! You want to be able to reward him for success, and his tolerance in the beginning will be minimal. Doing circles at the start will help to calm the mule, because he is not faced with any "wide-open spaces." When he becomes quiet and more confident, broaden your repertoire to actual patterns, all with your assistant on the lunge

Cindy Powell and Lucky Three Stardust, North Carolina State Fair, 1990. The well-trained driving mule is relaxed, confident, and dependable.

line and you driving from behind. Only after he has proved himself trustworthy (a couple of weeks at least) should you climb into the cart, and when you do, keep your assistant at his head for a little while longer! Review all previous driving patterns, adjusting them to accommodate the cart. When your mule can move calmly and easily through his patterns, hitched to the cart at the walk and the trot, you can go solo.

When you decide to go solo, have your assistant walk along with you for a ways, holding the lead line so that your mule will be in motion when he is released. Have your assistant detach the lead from the halter and continue to walk along with the mule the first time he is released. The next time, begin the same way, only have your assistant gradually walk farther away from the mule until the assistant becomes an observer. Your mule will hardly notice the assistant's absence if you approach this correctly and give your mule the time to learn before you ask him to go solo. Once he is confident when released, you can begin to work all of your driving patterns as before, only solo! Spend the time to get your mule used to each new step in driving. This will ensure safety and will greatly enhance your driving experience. Your mule will become a confident, obedient, and happy driving partner!

Lucky Three Mae Bea C.T.: The poles that you use may be too large to go through the shaft pulls on your harness. You can use a bungi cord on each side to hold your poles in place. Then tie the poles together with a rope. Use your draw-rein rigging in the beginning to give yourself more leverage with your mule. When you are walking your mule between the poles, keep your turns long and wide so that he does not become uncomfortable with the situation.

Once he has mastered the driving shafts, he will be ready to deal with the shafts on your breaking cart.

Lucky Three Mae Bea C.T.:
Again, when you first hitch to the cart, give yourself leverage with draw reins until you are sure how your mule will respond, even if he was quiet between the poles.

Guide him along the rail while you are behind, because this will give him a sense of direction and balance.

Walk and trot your mule through as many patterns and for as many days as it takes for him to become calm and accepting before you finally climb in.

Lucky Three Mae Bea C.T.:
Walk.

Trot.

Extended trot.

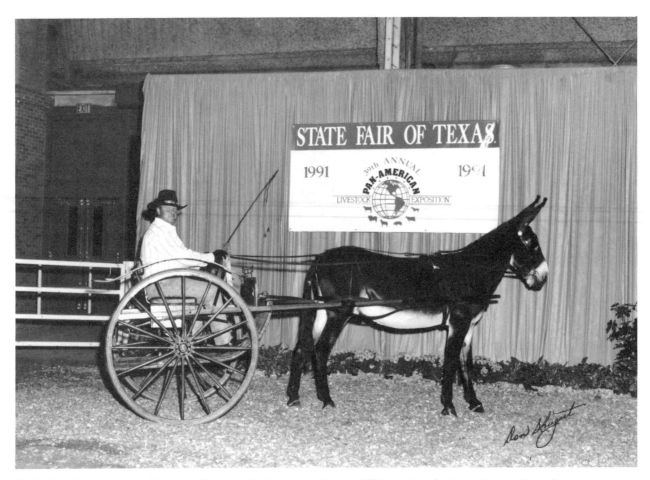

Eagle Rest Don Quixote, First Place Pleasure Driving. From Brayer Hill Farm, Boyd, Texas. Driver: Jim Joling.

CHAPTER XV

Judging the Driving Mule

Now that you have spent many months teaching your mule to drive and he is doing well, you decide that it might be fun to show him in harness. So, what does a judge look for in a driving class of mules? Well, it's basically the same as with horses.

The first and foremost consideration for a judge is your mule's manners, which will exhibit just how safe your mule is for driving. As with people, a judge can get an overall impression from the expression on your mule's face! An attentive and pleasant expression is definitely preferred. The expression reflects your mule's overall comfort within a situation. If he is comfortable, he responds to minimal aids calmly, confidently, and promptly. He backs up easily upon request, and he stands quietly at the halt with all four legs square. His ears are relaxed but attentively turned to the driver most of the time. Rapidly moving ears indicate tenseness and distraction.

A major contributing factor to your mule's overall manners is his conditioning. If your mule has been brought along with a carefully planned exercise program, his muscular growth and strength will increase with little or no stress, as with most athletes. The mule that is built up in this way has the strength to pull while maintaining a smooth, steady, effortless gait. Properly conditioned mules do not exhibit the tenseness that comes from overexertion, a tenseness that can inhibit the entire performance.

How can you tell if your mule is well-conditioned? Touch his body with your fingers at the neck, shoulders, barrel, loins, stifles, and rump. These muscles should be hard and not "mushy" to the touch. Stand behind your mule, and you should be able to see considerable gaskin development.

A driving class lasts approximately twenty to thirty minutes. If you condition your mule to medium trot for twenty minutes straight, without any sweating or hard breathing, he should be able to handle the class with no problem. Another helpful hint is to condition him on uneven ground; then, when he performs on the flat, it will seem a lot easier to him.

Meredith Hodges and Lucky Three Mae Bea C. T. in the Open Pleasure Driving at the Loveland Carriage Classic. Bea took third in a class of ten.

Condition your mule slowly to avoid over-exertion, muscular soreness, or injury. If you condition your mule beyond what is expected in the class, you won't have to worry about him being fit for the class. And, as long as he is well-conditioned, be sure that he is well-groomed as well.

Your mule's way of going is another important consideration for the judge. In the driving class, your mule will be asked for the walk, the collected trot, the working trot, and the rein back. The walk should be "regular and uncon-strained, energetic, but calm with even and determined steps with distinctively marked four equally spaced beats." In the collected trot, "the neck is raised, thus enabling the shoulders to move with greater ease in all directions, the hocks well-engaged and maintaining energetic impulsion notwithstanding the slower move-ment." The mule's steps are shorter but are lighter and more mobile. The working trot is a pace between the collected and extended trots. The mule "goes forward freely and straight, engaging the hindlegs with good hock action, on a taut, but light rein, the position being

balanced and unconstrained. The steps are even as possible and the hind feet touch the ground in the footprints of the forefeet." The rein back is "a kind of walk backwards. The legs being raised and set down simultaneously by diagonal pairs, the hindlegs remaining well in line and the legs being well raised." The mule that is conditioned slowly, with special attention given to straightness, balance, and bend, will begin to carry himself in good posture and will exhibit these true gaits naturally after a period of time.

The next consideration is the appropriate-ness of the animal to the vehicle that he is pulling. Never use a smaller mule to pull a large

Dena Hodges, Meredith Hodges, and Lucky Three Mae Bea C.T., Loveland Carriage Classic Youth Driving.

Meredith Hodges and Lucky Three Mae Bea C.T. showed that mules are not to be taken lightly when competing against horses!

Meredith Hodges tosses the ball in the bucket while Mae Bea C.T. stands quietly and waits.

Wheeling around in the Gambler's Choice class, where Mae Bea C.T. beats seven different breeds of horses!

Meredith Hodges and Lucky Three Mae Bea C.T. compete against horses with finesse in the Drive & Ride at the Loveland Carriage Classic, 1989.

Initiation from the hindquarters makes for a nice ground-covering walk under saddle.

Straightness, balance, suppleness, and rhythm give the mule a real edge against horses in the same class.

A quiet and steady Lucky Three Mae Bea C.T. wins second place in the Loveland Carriage Classic Drive & Ride class!

wagon, nor use a larger draft mule to pull a pony cart. Select a vehicle that pulls easily for your mule and one that is proportionate to his size. The overall picture should be balanced and harmonious. Fifty percent of your total class score will include your mule's manners, his conditioning, his way of going, and the appropriateness of the general turnout.

Twenty percent of your total score is determined from you, the whip or teamster. Hold your hands at waist level, about three inches in front of your body and about ten inches apart. "A rein passes between the forefinger and middle finger of each hand and is held secure with pressure from the thumb; the whip is held in the right hand." Always sit in good posture, and use your aids almost imperceptibly. An expert reinsman rarely exceeds a twelve-inch imaginary box around his hands.

Your dress should be appropriate to the vehicle in which you ride. For instance, a formal coach would require a more formal dress than would a two-wheel country cart. Dress must be conservative for the times. Western dress is permitted where appropriate. Hat, gloves, coat, tie, and a lap apron are required. A whip must be held in the hand at all times! Always look where you are going, check the judge for instructions periodically, and pay attention to spacing in the arena.

Lucky Three mules.

The remaining considerations for a judge are the vehicle and the harness, with each carrying 15 percent of your total score. The vehicle should be in good repair and of an appropriate size and style for your mule. It should fit him properly through the shafts and tugs. The harness should fit him as well as possible. Often, it is difficult to find horse harness to fit the lighter and smaller mules properly. You can approximate the size you need (i.e., pony, cob, horse, draft), however, then make the necessary adjustments or have a professional harness-maker help you.

Your mule should be fastened snugly to the vehicle. Be sure that your collar, or breast collar, fits your mule properly, because this can create soreness and make for a very unhappy mule. Adjust the breeching snugly enough to make your "brakes" effective. One of the most common mistakes made by beginning drivers is adjusting the breeching too loosely. This makes it difficult for your mule to slow down or to back up straight and evenly. The resulting slack will make his transitions look abrupt and awkward.

The driving judge must consider a lot, but he or she is also a human being, and basically, the judge is going to select those mules for placement in the class that he or she would most like to drive. If you follow the guidelines described here, your mule will be one of the judge's favorites.

Cindy Powell and Lucky Three Stardust place first at the North Carolina State Fair in Single Hitch Driving.

PRO PHOTO
Pam Olsen

Meredith Hodges and Lucky Three Firestorm, Utah State Fair Grand Champion Green English Mule, 1989.

Lucky Three Cyclone exhibits some of the natural beauty and grace of the mule.

Previous page: Lucky Three Pantera, foaled June 7, 1986.

Lucky Three Mae Bea C.T. and Ciji.

PRO PHOTO
Pam Olsen

Brayer Hill Othello, from Brayer Hill Farm, Boyd, Texas.

Lucky Three Sundowner: An excellent saddle mule head.

Dena Hodges on Lucky Three Ciji and Meredith Hodges on Lucky Three Mae Bea C.T. practice Pas De Deux over jumps.

Dena, Meredith, and Gary Hodges and Little Jack Horner, Loveland (Colorado) Christmas Parade, 1989.

Meredith Hodges and Lucky Three Mae Bea C.T. at the Abbe Ranch Horse Trials, Larkspur, Colorado, Novice Division 1992, Second Place.

Lucky Three Mae Bea C.T. not only jumps the jumps, but helps build them as well.

Brayer Hill Razzle Dazzle, from Brayer Hill Farm, Boyd, Texas.

Mules can be quite large!

And quite colorful!

Meredith Hodges and Lucky Three Mae Bea C.T., Loveland
Carriage Classic, 1989.

Dena and Meredith Hodges and Lucky Three Mae Bea C.T.
showed third in the Youth Pleasure Turnout and Youth
Working Pleasure classes.

Diane and Grace of Africa at George Lake, Republic of South Africa.

Above: Bob Talmadge and Dena Hodges with Rivers, originator of the mule-powered push vehicles.

Left: Blue Zebulon crashing a picnic. *Joan S. Byrne Photography.*

CHAPTER XVI

Training to Saddle

The ground-work for training a mule for harness or saddle is the same. His lessons in ground-work will allow him to learn restraint, submission, and balance while retaining the stature and mental stability of a confident and reliable animal. When your mule is responding obediently in the drive lines and through patterns and around obstacles, it is time to introduce him to the additional weight of the rider. Again, do this slowly and methodically.

At this point in training, your mule is acquainted with your directions coming from both sides of his body, from the front, and from behind. He must now become accustomed to receiving directions from his back (or over his head). First, however, he must learn to adjust his body to your additional weight.

After reviewing all of your ground-work lessons, detach the drive lines and use your bridle reins. Ask your mule to stand quietly while you grasp the saddle at the horn and cantle and boost yourself in a hanging position from his side. If he spooks and bolts away, let go of the saddle, maintain your hold on the left rein so as not to lose him, and quietly ask him again to "Whoa." When he does, try again. When he finally stands still for this, reward him lavishly, then put him away.

The next time out, review your lessons, including hanging off the saddle on the near side (mounting side), then go to the other side and do the same. When he stands quietly for this on both sides, you can proceed to the next step. It is always important to review what he has already learned so that his confidence will be maintained and his fear will be lessened. Take as long as you need for each step to be sure that he is truly comfortable with what he has learned.

It is advisable to have an assistant for the next stage in saddle training. Have your assistant stand at the mule's head and hold him while you review your "saddle hanging." If your mule is compliant, put your foot into the stirrup and slowly hoist yourself aboard, dragging your right leg against his body firmly. Move your leg gently up his hip, over his rump, and down the other side to the stirrup. If this does not disturb him, rock your weight from side to side and let him feel how the saddle

99

moves on his back. Reassure him continually during this procedure by touching him gently all over his body—wherever you can reach from this position. The more movement he can tolerate while standing still, the better he will do later. Do only as much of this in any one lesson as he can tolerate easily. Always try to end your lessons on a positive note, and do not get in too much of a hurry—that's usually where the trouble begins.

It is easy to get excited when you first mount your mule and he responds well. It is tempting to just allow him to walk off with you aboard. Fifteen years of experience has taught me, however, that the animal is not always completely aware of where you are the first few times aboard, and he can easily and very quickly come unglued. Thus, it is important to make him fully aware of what is actually happening by taking your time.

When your mule is quiet about your being on board, the last lesson, after review, is to have your assistant walk your mule a few steps while you ride. Each lesson, your mule should be required to walk a little farther until he is going calmly and deliberately. With your assistant leading the mule at a walk with a halter rope, begin to gently turn your mule and ask him to "Whoa" with the reins. Be sure to use exactly the same terminology that you have used throughout his ground-work to avoid any confusion. Above all, *do not forget to praise him* when he does well.

Next, have your assistant attach a lunge line to the halter and begin walking at the mule's head as before, only have your assistant walk a circle. As the mule circles, have your assistant slowly let out the lunge line so that the mule begins to walk more on his own while your assistant works his way slowly to the center

Lorraine Travis, founder and honorary secretary of the British Mule Society, with Frances, 14.2 hands, and Muffin, 11 hands, both dark bays. *Photo courtesy of Farmers Weekly.*

of the circle. Guide your mule around the circle with the reins. The first time or two, ask your mule only to walk. When he is quiet and stable at the walk, move on to the trot, but be sure to first work both ways at the walk.

Keep your assistant on hand throughout this stage until your mule will walk, trot, canter, and back up on the lunge line. The assistant acts to prevent extreme resistance or a possible blow-up. He is there to help the mule toward success and can also prevent you from being injured.

Mules usually get through this stage of training fairly rapidly, and most won't buck until they are asked to canter. Most mules will buck at the canter if the rider's weight is shifted too far forward. This is also when most mules can lose a saddle over their head! If your mule does decide to buck, verbalize a firm "No" after calling his name to get his attention. Let him stop, check your saddle for anything that could cause this reaction, then mount and try again. When a horse bucks, you usually urge him on to a smooth canter, but with a mule it is different. The mule lacks a good set of withers, and so most problems arise because of saddle position. If you urge him on, you may only compound the problem. Your mule will appreciate the fact that you took the time to check, even if the problem wasn't the saddle. When he does canter nicely, be generous with your praise, saying, "Good Boy (or Girl)" with every stride to let him know that this is indeed what you expect. Then, if you have to say "No," he will clearly understand what you mean. If you take the time to do this before riding off alone with your mule, he will be much more attentive and obedient when you move on to his basic saddle training, and the life that you save may be your own!

Vinesse and Lucky Three Midnight Victory, Anglo-Trakehner mare and mule.

Lucky Three Calypso: If you have mounted him as a young mule before lunging training, he most likely will stay quiet for this procedure. If he has not been mounted previously, take your time and don't actually put all of your weight on him until he is calm and relaxed. Feed him treats and encourage him to see, feel, and accept this strange situation.

Equines are most definitely two-sided, and what is done on one side should always be repeated on the other to assure mental and physical balance and stability.

When he is calm enough to handle all of your weight over his back, stroke his body as far as you can reach in front and behind. He needs to learn not to be startled by touch from his back. When mounting and dismounting, slip your leg over his rump and ask him to stand quietly while your leg bumps and rubs him. This keeps him from jumping forward if you accidently bump him in the future.

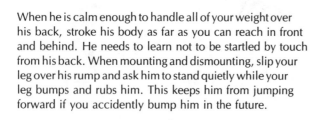

Holding onto his neck for balance, rock the saddle back and forth while praising him to stand still.

Reward him for being so calm and accepting. If he doesn't appear to be bothered by this, go ahead and encourage him to walk a few steps. Always take your feet out of the stirrups before dismounting to avoid getting your foot caught. A treat is definitely in order after a first run when your mule is as successful as this boy has been. When you are back on the ground, be sure to take the time to let your mule know how truly pleased you are with him and with his performance. Lots of love and affection go a long way with longears!

Lucky Three Foxfire: Ground-driving, as shown here, is a good relaxation technique.

Doing this exercise each day before you mount your very green mules will help them to relax and accept your seat more easily.

To teach your mule to back up, first push him back in the chest with your hand while pulling back on the reins, and give the verbal command to back.

Next, pull alternately on the reins as shown, and give the verbal command to back up.

Mount your mule for the first few times only when he is standing very calmly.

Praise him for maintaining a calm attitude.

There are lots of little patterns and directional changes that can be done in the round pen.

Meredith and Gary Hodges with Lucky Three Firestorm and Cyclone, Utah State Fair, 1989.

CHAPTER XVII

English or Western— Dressage Means "Training"

Why does dressage training lend itself so well to training mules? This question can be answered only by understanding what dressage really means and how it pertains to the mule's mental and physical development and to your own expectations. When most people think of dressage, they picture the elegant Lipizanners of the Spanish Riding School in Vienna, Austria. It is easy to perceive dressage as a more advanced form of horsemanship; however, this type of dressage is the result of many years of intense training. It is also easy to believe that this is not the activity in which most people see themselves competing! It requires much more developed skills from the rider, and the movements exhibited are not generally employed in the practical use of animals. Goals are perceived as unattainable for the common horseman, and dressage training is discarded for more commercial techniques that seem to give more simple and immediate results in the English, Western, and gaming mules. Understanding the beginning levels of dressage might help to explain why dressage really is a preferred way to train when considering the mental and physical well-being of mules.

At first glance, the training-level patterns may seem entirely too simple and pointless to the average rider. A reining pattern is much more inviting because it is stimulating and exciting. Think about this more carefully, however, and you will realize that reining can be mentally and physically stressful on the young mule unless he is brought along slowly and carefully. The mule is strong and capable of running through any type of bridle arrangement, which means that you want to avoid as much resistance as possible. My mules exhibit resistive behavior when they are confused or frightened, but never out of pure stubbornness.

It is often taken for granted that since a young mule can walk, trot, canter, and back up by himself, he should be able to do this with a person astride. Young mules, however, are born with as diverse postures as are children, and few will exhibit good posture without being reminded constantly. People compensate continually for deficiencies in their body structure, and posture varies from situation to situation.

For example, a person may sit straight in a straight-backed chair, but the sinking comfort of a plush couch will produce a collapsed posture that eventually may produce a sore back and neck muscles. The mule will also sacrifice his good posture to accommodate an unbalanced and inexperienced rider.

In the simplicity of the training-level patterns, the issue of good posture can be addressed, and the necessary muscles for maintaining good posture can be conditioned. In the training-level patterns, a judge will always look for the same things: "a willing, obedient mount who moves forward freely, responding to the rider's aids and accepting the bit." Your mule will be encouraged to maintain the best possible posture for his individual stage of development while you practice the same. The simpleness of the patterns will enable you to minimize losses of balance by either of you. As the muscles are strengthened and conditioned, the mule will be better able to carry his own body and yours; only then should you begin to

Lucky Three Desirée, Cody Ann Watson, Florida State Fair, February 1991.

Lucky Three Desirée, Cody Ann Watson, Florida State Fair, February 1990.

ask for more engagement in the hindquarters toward more collection. By taking the time to condition and strengthen muscles, your mule gains physical exercise that is not taxing and painful; thus, his mental attitude remains fresh and happy. By conditioning your mule in a carefully sequenced pattern of exercises, you more often avoid the possibility of throwing him off-balance and into the confusion and fear that lead to resistance and disobedience.

With your own posture in mind, you can develop rider and mule as one unit. The process is slow but thorough and mutually satisfying. The dressage saddle itself allows the stability of a saddle, yet gives the closest possible contact with your mule's body (other than bareback), making your leg and seat cues far more clear and perceptible to your mule. With more clearly defined cues, the mule is better able to discern your wishes without fear or resistance.

Western saddles are used more universally for training, but much of this is to accommodate riders with limited ability. Use plays an important part in the breaking saddle used, but many trainers today agree that the least amount of equipment used in the beginning is probably best. The Western saddle may certainly be used for breaking. From the mule's standpoint, however, there is a lot of leather between you and your mule that can cause interference in communication. If the mule cannot "feel" his rider well, a leg or rein cue can come as a surprise and produce resistance. For this reason, I prefer to start training in an all-purpose, or dressage, saddle. Still, I recommend training in a Western saddle for the less-experienced rider.

In training-level dressage, movements are limited to straight lines, simple transitions (i.e., walk to trot, trot to canter, canter to trot, trot to walk, and trot and walk to halt), and large,

twenty-meter circles. This allows you to spend time working on rhythm, regularity, and cadence in all three gaits. You can also work on overall obedience to the aids, steadiness, and bending of your mule's body from head to tail through corners while maintaining an upright posture. This allows your mule the time to properly condition his muscles and learn to stay between the aids in a comfortable and relaxed manner. He learns to move freely and to go forward easily while you develop your own muscles and perfect your technique. Stress is at a minimum.

As in any exercise program, it is not advisable to drill and repeat every day. As with

Judy Temple and Lucky Three Twilight prepare for their first Dressage Test in New Hampshire.

Gary Hodges and Lucky Three Cyclone practice Green Western Pleasure at the Lucky Three Ranch in Loveland, Colorado, 1988.

Meredith Hodges and Lucky Three Mae Bea C.T., Colorado Classic Horse Show, 1987.

Even Dressage mules enjoy a nice long day in the Rocky Mountains trail riding. Just like people, the mule enjoys his relaxation and can then do his work more happily.

any athlete, muscles need to be exercised, then allowed rest for a day or two to avoid serious injury. In between dressage days, take your mule for a simple trail ride or just let him rest. The time off and the variety will keep him fresh and attentive. Three times a week usually is sufficient with dressage training for proper development and conditioning, with two days of simple hacking, or trail riding, and two days of rest. This also takes the pressure off of you. If you don't feel like riding a particular day, you won't feel that you must, because your mule will retain his learning better without the added stress of drilling day after day. Try to think of your mule's training in terms of yourself. Would you care to be drilled to exhaustion day after day? How would you feel mentally and physically if you did?

Dressage is training, basic through the most advanced. It is thoughtful, considerate, and kind and will produce a mule mentally and physically capable of doing anything that you might like with a relaxed and willing attitude. It may take a little longer, but the results speak for themselves.

Meredith Hodges and Lucky Three Firestorm, Utah State Fair Grand Champion Green English Mule, 1989.

Diane and Grace of Africa, Dressage competition, George Riding Club, George, South Africa, 1991.

PRO PHOTO
Pam Olsen

Meredith Hodges and Lucky Three Firestorm, Utah State Fair Green English Champion Mule.

CHAPTER XVIII

Proper Conditioning through Balance

Your mule, up to this point, has learned his basic commands (Walk, Trot, Canter, Back, Haw, and Gee), how to balance his body through the gaits, and how to respond in a calm, sensible manner. The introduction of your weight on his back was made while he was still on the lunge line to facilitate his success and to minimize his fear and resistance. When he is calm and certain about you aboard with him on the lunge line, you can give him more responsibility by eliminating the lunge line.

It is important at this stage that you fully understand the implications of the training to come. Not only are you teaching your mule certain movements, but you also are conditioning his body to perform these movements easily. Animals are too often asked to do certain exercises before they are physically capable of doing them. Failure to perform the desired movement usually produces frustration in both mule and rider, leading ultimately to extreme resistance. This resistance, in turn, causes the animal to become sore, uncomfortable, and unwilling to perform. The mule's time with his trainer ceases to be a pleasant, rewarding experience. This animal "learns" to be stubborn and unwilling through no real fault of his own.

Mules mature much more slowly than horses, and their knees fuse about six months later than those of a horse. In order to maintain a rider, a mule must have the mental ability to handle longer attention spans, and his body must be physically capable of carrying the extra weight. This does not usually occur until he has reached his third birthday. I have ridden two-year-olds in the past, and they seem to handle my light body weight alright for short periods of time. I have found, however, that they simply do not possess the mental capacity to really "learn." I consequently found myself teaching the same exercises for two years that should really have taken only one year. Better to go slowly and wait that extra year.

If you have followed the training procedures outlined thus far, your mule should be close to three years old at this point anyway. The lunging and ground-driving that you have done will have built the muscles that your mule needs to carry your weight efficiently. The commands and cues that he has learned will have built his confidence in himself and in you.

To begin, define your goals clearly. You are conditioning an athlete, which means that too much stress and undue strain will only defeat your purpose. Your mule must learn to travel in a balanced, rhythmic, and forward fashion while staying between your aids (hands and legs) and must remain responsive to your seat. The walk should be a clear, four-beat marching pace, well-marked and well-maintained; the trot, a two-beat diagonal pace with a moment of suspension, unconstrained and elastic; and the canter, a light, cadenced, three-beat pace with a moment of suspension.

At all of these gaits, you should have the sensation that your mule is riding "uphill," or from back to front, with the hindquarters initiating the action. It is difficult to attain this

Little Jack Horner.

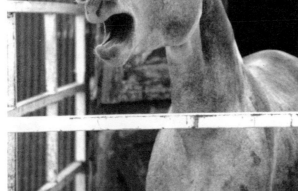

proper frame. Trainers too often sacrifice proper frame to attain a slower speed, resulting in an animal that will throw his weight on the forehand and thus appear to be traveling downhill. With patience and deliberate training, your mule can be taught to shift his weight backward and to initiate his movements from the hindquarters, thus keeping his body in good posture and balance and making his movements more fluid and effortless.

My beginning exercise facilitates the responsiveness and physical development of your mule at all three gaits concurrently. The first pattern is shaped like an hourglass. Place four cones in the four corners of your arena. Leave plenty of room to go between them and the rail. Place two cones in the center of the arena and space them about eight feet apart. Begin the pattern by tracking along the rail on the short side of the arena. When you reach the corner, go around the cone, then through the cones in the center. Go back to the rail on the same side, around the next cone, and along the rail on the short side of the arena to the next cone. Proceed around it, then through the center cones again, and on to the next cone on the same side. Return to the short side where you began. You will go around the cones, but you will not "circle" them.

Begin this pattern at a walk, using light contact on the bit. Let your own body rock with the rhythm of your mule's body. As he steps out with the right front leg, allow your hand and leg on the same side to follow his front leg. Do the same on the left side, alternating sides with every stride. If your mule is a little slow, push him on with your leg. If he does not respond adequately to your leg, use a riding crop. If he tends to be a little speedy, hesitate following his leg for a split second during each stride. *Do not*, however, *inhibit his forward motion* by alternating pressure directly against his body; this may cause resistance and inhibit training.

As your mule rounds the cones, ask him to keep his body upright and to bend to the arc of the turn rather than allowing him to drop his inside shoulder and fall *into* the turn. You can do this by maintaining a straight neck with the outside rein. Pull your inside rein straight back toward your hip appropriate to the degree of the turn, while your inside leg is at the girth for support and your outside leg is sufficiently behind the girth on his barrel for impulsion. The connection that you should begin to feel is from your inside leg to your outside rein, and the sensation that you should feel is an upright mule around the turn.

After you round the corner, you will be approaching the center cones. Halfway between the corner and the center cones is an evident change of direction. At this point, even your hands and legs, and sit as if to halt, but don't stop—just change your hands and legs appropriate to the new direction.

After passing through the center, you are again faced with a new direction toward the next corner cone. Halfway between the center and the next corner, even your hands and legs again, and sit as if to halt, then move your aids appropriately for the new direction. This is the beginning of what is known as the "half-halt," or "call to balance." It allows your mule the time to balance himself for the new movement.

This pattern can be done at the walk and at the trot. Pay special attention to your own position and to your mule's responsiveness. Try to ride the pattern as accurately as you could draw it, making smooth, gradual arcs and straight lines where needed. Avoid sharp turns and crooked lines as much as possible. In the trot, it often helps to post as in English to help clarify directional changes for your mule. Your "call to balance," or "half-halt," will come when you sit two beats to change your posting diagonal. To vary the pattern a little and to prevent utter boredom, add large circles on one end of your arena, using half of the pattern to outline your circle. Do not attempt small circles at this stage; it is physically too much to ask of your mule at a pace any faster than a walk.

Use your large (fifty-foot) circle for your canter work. As you canter, maintain a straight neck with the outside rein, and use the inside rein to determine the arc of the circle. Support your mule's body on the inside with your leg at the girth while your outside leg, behind the girth, propels him forward. Allow your hands to go out with his head while your legs reach down and back toward the ground. When his

head comes back to you for the next stride, use this time only to check him for the next stride. At this point, your legs will be wrapped tightly around him, and his body will be in total suspension and uninhibited. To deepen your seat, think, "Down . . . and . . . down . . . and . . . down" for your legs with every stride. Hold your hands evenly and together, and make a circular motion down with his head, then up and back toward you. Practice coordinating your hands and legs with his motion. Your hands go out with his front legs and head as your legs go down; then, your hands and legs "close" on him as you are in suspension, which is a call to balance at this stage in training. Do not worry if he is a little fast to start, because he will slow down when he meets no resistance.

Pay attention to these special details at this stage of training, and you will greatly enhance your mule's ability to perform. You will also develop your own riding skills. Taking the time to develop muscles and improve coordination will make more difficult movements a lot easier at a later time.

Judy Rose and Sweetwater Laverne.

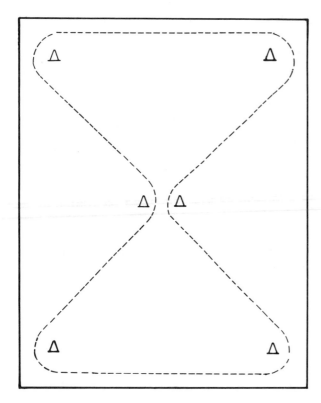

Left: The hourglass pattern is a good pattern to use for facilitating good balance in the young mule.
Above: Use cones! An arena without cones is like a house without furniture.

Concentrate on straightness and balance around the cones and on maintaining rhythm and cadence of your mule's gait.

When you ride your mule in the open for the first time, allow him to look around a little before you ask him to go to work.

Start by asking him to walk straight lines and diagonal patterns, lengthening and shortening the walk. Keep your hands even to promote straightness through the head and neck between your hands.

Allow some slack in the reins to start. Let him come on to the bit in good time.

When he is ready to begin going on the bit, he will be more submissive on his own, and his halts will become more square.

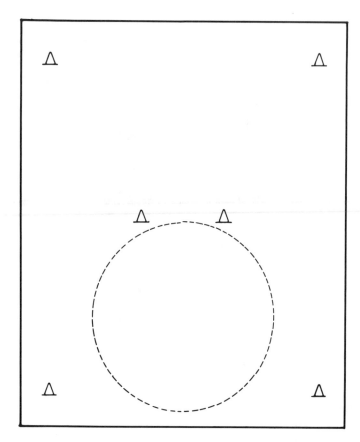

The canter circle for the young mule in the beginning should be rather large to facilitate the best balance for him. The diameter of the circle should be approximately forty-five to sixty feet.

You can encourage him to flex at the poll by giving gentle tugs as you round your circles.

If he starts to veer off-course, pull your rein back toward your hip, and not to the inside, to maintain good balance.

Keeping your hands in close and even will help him to balance his body at the canter; keep your elbows flexible and your hands and legs pushing him forward. As he gains strength, his canter will slow, so don't worry if he is a little fast at first. Always look where you are going.

PRO PHOTO
Pam Olsen

Dena Hodges and Lucky Three Mae Bea C.T., Utah State Fair Champion Youth Pleasure, Showmanship and Trail.

CHAPTER XIX

Moving Off of Your Legs

When your mule first learns the hourglass pattern discussed in Chapter 18, you will feel his balance shifting from one side to the other as he anticipates changes. As he becomes familiar with the pattern, this "snaky" sensation begins to dissipate, and new balancing problems begin to arise. He most likely will begin to speed up on the straightaways and find something to shy away from on the corners. This is simply your mule's way of telling you that he is ready to accept more responsibility for his body movements. He has learned that you want him to travel forward; now he must learn how to travel forward with good rhythm, cadence, lateral balance, and bend.

In order for your mule to understand these concepts, you must teach him to pay more attention to seat and leg cues. You can do this with a few simple exercises.

He needs to realize that you wish for him to move away from leg pressure and to slow down when you sink your weight into the saddle and put pressure on the reins. To teach this, first walk a large circle, then halt beside the fence. Your mule should be standing exactly parallel to the fence. His first new movement is to turn on the forehand; that is, he keeps the front legs stationary while the hind legs complete the turn. To get him to do this, turn his face slightly to the fence, then kick behind the girth on the same side. Keep your contact on both reins throughout the turn. The instant he is again parallel to the fence, release the pressure on the reins and send him forward to walk the circle again.

At first, his turns will be awkward and sometimes incomplete, but if you are slow and deliberate about positioning and quick with your rein release, he will soon learn to turn properly. When he is relatively proficient at the fence, begin stopping anywhere along the circle and encourage the turn without the aid of the fence. When you do a turn in the open, be sure that the leg opposite your "kicking" leg is ready to stop him from turning too far. Ask him to do these turns from a walk, a trot, and a canter on the circle. Remember, though, that in order to facilitate smoothness and fluidity through the transitions, you must allow your mule to go through the

121

gaits to the halt (i.e., canter to trot to walk) and wait for him to settle before you ask for the turn.

Now that he is beginning to understand the concept of moving away from your leg, it is time to ask him to engage the front quarters at the request of your hands. In this next exercise, ask him to move around a designated center on a circle like the spoke of a wheel. Mark a spot in the center of your arena, then move out from it about thirty to forty feet and point your mule directly at your mark in the center.

Ask your mule to move his shoulders over by gently squeezing your direct rein; he will start to turn in that direction. Let him take one step with each front foot. Stop, then ask him to move his hindquarters over one step by giving leg nudges behind the girth as you did for the turn on the forehand. When he complies, praise him and let him know in no uncertain terms that he has done well.

Keep moving around your center in this manner, and be sure to do this exercise both ways. As he begins to understand more clearly what is being asked, you will be able to use your hand and leg cues simultaneously and his lateral movement will become more smooth and fluid. Understand that this is not a side pass, because your mule is, in fact, moving forward along a circle. Be careful that his leading legs (front and back) are crossing over in front of the other legs and not behind. If he were doing a true side pass, he would not be on the circle for very long. After these two exercises are mastered, your mule should begin to understand the meaning behind the use of your legs.

I mentioned at the beginning of the chapter that your mule might speed up and hesitate at the corners. He does this because he is losing his balance and must compensate somehow. Now that he understands the meaning of legs, you will be able to help him maintain his balance more effectively. Keeping his body erect in circles and around turns will condition his muscles evenly and properly and will keep him more balanced. It also will develop his confidence, and your mule will become more rhythmic and cadenced. See for yourself . . .

Take your mule back to the hourglass pattern and add about a thirty-foot circle at each cone. Starting at the short end of your arena, track forward and around the first cone. Hold your inside leg firmly at the girth while your outside leg rhythmically nudges the mule around the circle behind the girth. At the same time, keep your hands even and your thumbs up. In rhythm with your outside leg, squeeze/release your inside (or direct) rein to indicate the direction of the turn for your mule's shoulders. Do not try to turn his head to the inside of the circle, because this will cause his shoulder to "pop out" of the circle. Keep his head directly in front of his shoulders by keeping your hands even and reasonably close together. As he comes out of the circle and onto the straightaway, sit squarely over your mule with even hands and legs. Sink your weight down into the saddle as if to halt, but don't stop. As quickly as you become square, reposition your hands and legs for the new bend on the next circle at the center cone. Complete that circle, straighten, then move on to the next corner and on around in the same fashion. Do your pattern a few times each way, then go back and do it again without the circles. Your mule will work more smoothly after these lateral and bending exercises.

After a couple of months of these exercises, your mule should improve greatly in cadence, rhythm, and balance, and his forward movement should become more solid and less frantic. He will be much more relaxed, calm, and willing to please, because he is being conditioned slowly and evenly. If your cues are clear and humane, your mule will soon learn to go "on the bit" basically on his own accord, because this will be the most comfortable frame in which to be.

Start your turn by holding the right rein steady, open the right leg, then give little tugs on the left rein while you nudge him behind the girth with your left leg. Just reverse for a turn the other direction.

As he steps around, try to control each step and keep your own body erect and aiding.

If his hindquarters start to stick, just pull his nose around a little more, but be careful not to turn his head too much to the side.

The last couple of steps, work to straighten his head and neck and get a little flexion and roundness to his body.

Then send him forward from his last step to maintain forward movement and balance.

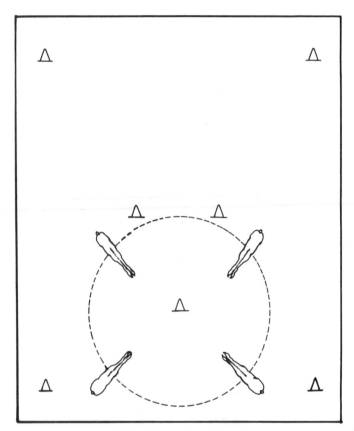

In the lateral wheel, your mule learns to listen to your legs and seat and their indications toward lateral control of the mule's body.

When doing the lateral wheel, be sure to take it slowly, one step at a time. Feel your body weight shift with that of your mule, sit up straight with your weight shifted back, give light cues with the reins, and focus your eyes on the cone in the center. If you run into trouble, just stop, settle your mule, then straighten him out. Begin the lateral movement again. Above all, do not let yourself force the motion, because this is easy to do when things are right! If things are not going right, take time to regroup and then go on.

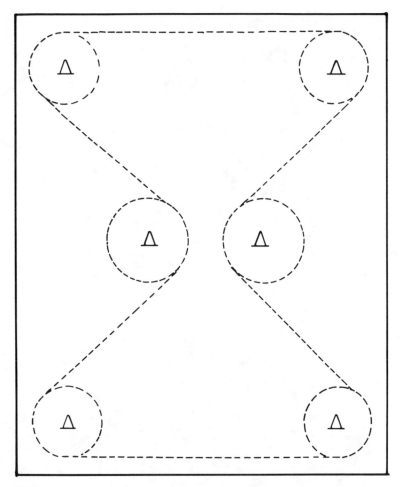

Circling the cones through the hourglass pattern helps the young mule to further collect his balance through turns. It will also increase his responsiveness to your aids.

Meredith Hodges and Lucky Three Ciji, I.S.S.O. Champion Mule, 1991, waiting for the signal to back in the sidesaddle class.

CHAPTER XX

Rein Back

Many training techniques used today work well on either horses or mules, and less technique and a more direct approach works with donkeys. In the case of "backing," however, the problems are universal. Some equine individuals seem to back up more easily than others. There *are* some similarities within equine species regarding difficult animals. Horses that are resistant to backing either shake their head violently from side to side or rear up and try to throw themselves over backwards. Resistant mules try to walk sideways or forward, and resistant donkeys are either stone statues or terrific leaners! All of these tendencies pose serious problems for the trainer.

Before teaching an equine to back up, you must understand the animal's body mechanics and his mental attitude to get the best results. Backing is a reverse, two-beat, diagonal gait. When backing straight, the equine is unable to see what is directly behind him; however, he can see peripherally on both sides. The depth perception of an equine is questionable anyway, but when an equine must perceive the reverse, his vision is even more impaired. This causes the animal to become tense when he is asked to back up, because he must trust his trainer not to back the equine's precious little rear into anything that might hurt him! If the trainer has been even a little abusive in the past, the equine will not be able to trust and will become resistant. On the other hand, if the animal has been brought along well and is being asked to back up on the long lines, he may not want to "back over" the trainer. The trainer could perceive this as disobedience. When asked to back up under saddle, still more problems can arise.

In order to back up straight and smoothly, the equine must be able to lower his head, round his back, and step back easily, with the power of his backing shifted from his hindquarters to his center of gravity over his back. If the rider has not prepared his equine for the back up by allowing the animal to round under his seat, the animal will be resistant. The animal may raise his head and hollow his back, making it very difficult, at best, to perform the back up. If you have trouble visualizing

Meredith Hodges and Little Jack Horner, Bishop Mule Days, 1992.

this, get on your hands and knees and try it yourself—see how it feels!

Before you begin to back up, take that extra couple of seconds to prepare your animal. Alternately, squeeze your reins and ask him to lower his head a little (not too much at first!). Keep your legs snugly around his barrel, and lift your seat ever so slightly by leaning forward a little. Check over your shoulder to be sure that he won't back into anything. Then, with corresponding rein and leg, squeeze and release alternately from side to side: first, right rein, right leg; then, left rein, left leg. By pulling on first one side and then the other, you actually allow him to see more directly behind, thus eliminating much of the apprehension that he feels when he cannot see. Pretend that you are pushing him backward with your legs, directly after giving a gentle tug on the corresponding rein. In the beginning, be satisfied with one or two steps and praise him.

Do this exercise in a two-beat fashion, with the rein tug coming only a split second sooner than the corresponding leg. This prevents the

hindquarters from resisting, and it is here where most resistance in backing originates. If you pull both reins at the same time, the hindquarters are not affected and may cause considerable resistance! Animals that learn to back up correctly eventually learn to back up on a mere tug of the reins, but this is not the way to start.

Horses and mules learn to back up more easily than donkeys. Why go backward when you can turn around to go forward?! As agile as donkeys are, this is not such a far-out way to think. If a donkey tried to turn around on a narrow trail with a rider aboard, however, his balance could be affected severely. Chances are, the donkey would make it, but the rider wouldn't! The donkey needs to learn to back upon command, because safety is of the utmost importance.

The simplest way to encourage your donkey to back up is to ride or drive him into a three-sided tie stall, where he has no way to escape but backward. Ask him to back up with the cues outlined, and praise him for each step backward. If you are ground driving, just alternate rein pressure while you step backwards. Keep your tugs on the reins minimal. Pulling on your donkey's mouth too much will only defeat your purpose. If your donkey is hitched to a vehicle, make sure that the weight that he has to push is not too heavy for him to manage. Adjust the breeching tightly enough so that your donkey can lean into it with his rear, and be sure that it is not so low that it will inhibit his upper hind legs.

If you have checked all of these factors and your donkey still will not back out of the stall, ask an assistant to wave a fearful object (such as a brightly colored scarf) low and in front of him. He should dip his head to focus on the object and begin to back up, at which time you can reward him. You have set up a situation in which you can predict that his reaction will be the correct one. Once he has done this a few times, he should begin to make the connection between your cues and his action. Always keep your cues gentle, but clear. Be prepared to praise those first one or two steps immediately, and don't ask for too many steps too soon! Just as an animal is conditioned to perform anything else, his body must also be conditioned to back up. Backing without conditioning those muscles can cause injury. Taking it slowly and cautiously diminishes the chance for resistance. Work up your speed in backing only after he is backing straight and easily. When he has had time off, be sure to take the time to recondition those muscles before asking for speed again!

I can't count the hours that I have spent sitting on board my donkey, waiting for a foot to move, giving the cue to just one side over and over again! Patience is the key to success with any animal, but with donkeys, it's a necessity. Be patient and deliberate with your training. Don't get upset, and don't try to be forceful. He has to move sometime! Even donkeys get bored standing in one place for too long!

Little Jack Horner jumping. Little Jack Horner is proud of his many accomplishments. He seems to think that anything the mules can do, so can he. At ten years of age, he is trained in most Western and English events and is working at 1st Level Dressage. He does spins, slides, and flying changes in Reining and is currently jumping 4 feet under saddle.

When teaching your donkey to back up, first put him into a space out of which he must back up. If he refuses to go in, use your assistant with the scarf or paper bag to encourage him forward into the space.

Once in the space, allow your donkey the time to settle before you give the cues to back up.

When he has settled, give the cue to back up by squeezing, then releasing, the reins slowly and rhythmically.

If he does not respond by backing up, have your assistant come in front of him with the scarf or bag and encourage him backward as you give the cues.

Alternate your rein pressure with the front legs as each leg steps backward.

When he has backed two or three steps, stop, praise him,

and let him relax a few minutes before you try again.

Performance is greatly enhanced in equines when the rider's aids are clear and polite, as shown here with Fran Howe and Blue Zebulon in the Donkey Pleasure Class at the Colorado Classic Horse Show.

CHAPTER XXI

Clarifying the Aids

After working in the hourglass pattern for a month or two, you should begin to notice improved balance and forward motion in your mule. His "snaky" way of going should be barely perceptible. Hesitation is at a minimum and has been replaced by a more confident forward motion. He is responsive to legs and seat, although his responses at this time may be somewhat delayed. This delay is due to the fact that he is still unsure about the complete function of your legs and seat. Let's look at it from the mule's point of view for a moment. It is clear that when a rein is pulled, that is the direction in which you go, and it is clear that while standing still, you move away from a nudging leg. But in motion, the rider's body (particularly the legs and the seat) is not so clearly understood due to the rider's momentary loss of balance. As you catch your own balance, you sometimes inadvertently cue the mule with your legs and seat. This can be confusing for the mule. To help clarify these cues, you can add a few more exercises to your program.

First, you must visualize and feel your *own* body moving along the ground like the body of your mule. Pretend that your legs are cut off at the knees, and allow your body, from your waist to your knees, to proceed in synchronization with your mule's front legs. As you begin to get this feeling, be aware of the mule's hind legs coming in under your seat with each stride, pushing your body and his forward. You should get the sensation that you are walking, trotting, or cantering along the ground on your knees. You will notice that as you ride, your pelvis and upper leg are always in motion, as is your mule, until you halt. In the halt, sit squarely, balanced, and motionless. Coordinating your own body movement with that of the mule will help your mule to understand better the function of your legs and seat.

At this point, you may need a riding crop to back up your leg cues. Your mule should move away from your leg (be it forward or laterally) upon a nudge, but if he does not, you don't want to get into a kicking match. If he does not respond on the first nudge, use your crop lightly just behind your leg to get his attention. Personally, I don't like to use spurs, because a mule may overreact to them and run

Meredith Hodges and Lucky Three Sundowner wait their turn for a 1st Level Dressage Test at Clearview Farms Dressage Schooling Show, where they placed second in a class of eight.

off with you. Once this happens, it is difficult to regain his trust and interest. What actually happens with spurs, more often than not, is that you initially cue your mule for the move, but the sharp dig of the spurs to back up the command actually startles him. He jumps, you lose your balance, and you inadvertently gig him again. You thus lose the clarity of your initial cue. You simply have more control over a crop than spurs, and it just makes more sense to take the path of least resistance.

Begin your exercises as described earlier through the hourglass pattern to warm up your mule. Then, just to break the monotony, introduce the serpentine. In the beginning, do your serpentines in three loops using your entire arena. Each loop of the serpentine will take up one-third of the arena. Start at the short end of the arena and move along an arc that will touch the tail of the long side one-fourth of the total distance, and continue in a symmetrical fashion to the one-half mark on the opposite long side. Then go back to the three-fourths mark on the first long side and finish the arc

along the short side of the arena. In the middle of the arena, at the one-third mark, reposition for the new bend, or change of direction. Always prepare a couple of strides before the center so that the actual change of bend occurs right at the center. The cues to your mule are exactly the same as they were in the hourglass pattern.

The serpentine pattern accomplishes a number of goals: It breaks your mule out of pattern learning, it reinforces all information learned within the pattern, and it promotes mule/rider rapport. With only two changes of direction in the serpentine, it further clarifies the concepts of submission and bending through the rider's aids.

To enhance the mule's response to seat, you can do yet another exercise. Perform the exercises along the rail to prevent balancing complications. Begin at the walk. Walk a few steps, stop, then back up a few steps. While you are doing this, pay special attention to your own body—walk along (with your seat and legs) with the mule, as if you were walking along the ground, halt, then walk backward. Do this

Meredith Hodges and Lucky Three Sundowner, 1990 Bishop Mule Days World Champion 2nd Level Dressage Mule!

exercise at the walk, the trot, and the canter, going both ways in the arena, and gradually shorten the distance between halts. Your mule will soon slow and stop as your seat becomes motionless. He may even remind you a time or two that your seat needs to move as he stops when you "supposedly" did not ask! Often times, as a rider you tend to sit apathetically when your mule begins to move correctly in order not to "mess him up," but if you do this, the harmony between your body and your mule's body is broken. You must train yourself as a rider to follow through the movements as you ask your mule to do. Then, when you do become motionless, so does your mule.

You can improve your own coordination and balance by practicing these exercises on the ground without your mule. For instance, trot a distance, then come to a halt. As you trot, feel your legs carried forward through your hip joint in a light, forward fashion. As you come into the halt, the downward motion in your hips becomes heavier, creating a heavier seat when aboard your mule. The seat is the heaviest at the halt when all of your weight is grounded. The looser and more flexible your own body, the more loose and flexible your mule's body will be. There is a direct relationship between corresponding body parts on both mule and rider, so you must constantly work on yourself as well as on your mule. By doing this, you facilitate the harmony of your own body with that of your mule, and you eventually create a picture of "oneness"—beautifully balanced and pleasingly fluid.

Lucky Three Mae Bea C.T., 1991 World Champion Jumping Mule, Bishop Mule Days, California.

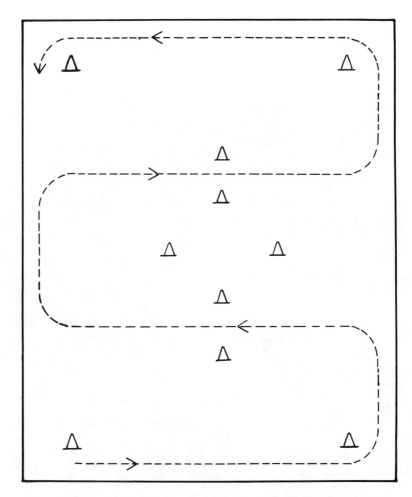

The serpentine will help the young mule to maintain his balance through a change of direction while also maintaining a cadenced and rhythmic gait.

Meredith Hodges and Lucky Three Mae Bea C.T. practice cross-country at Lory State Park in Fort Collins, Colorado.

CHAPTER XXII

Facilitating Balance and Harmony

As your seat and legs become more effective in cueing your mule, you will begin to feel more of a connection between his body and your own. At this time, you need to begin to let your mule take more responsibility for his own balance and response with subtle cues. It is sometimes difficult to assess just how much your mule is relying on your legs and hands to direct him and keep him erect. In order to shift this responsibility from you to him, minimize your cues so that they become indications rather than demands. This requires a certain amount of trust between you and your mule. The exercises here will add to your training repertoire and will help to facilitate that trust and further develop the harmony of balance between you and your mule.

After you have reviewed your previous lessons with your mule through the hourglass pattern, circles, and serpentines, allow him to walk and rest on a long rein for awhile. When he is free from tension, direct him back into the hourglass pattern, using only your seat and legs. Leave the reins draped on his neck, and cross your arms in front of your chest. Sit squarely over your mule's back on the straightaways. As you begin the arc of a circle, turn your upper body from the waist in the direction of the circle, keeping your eyes focused on the arc of your circle about twenty to thirty feet in front of your mule. Let your eyes always follow ahead in this manner. Your outside leg is your "impulsing" leg, ever driving the mule forward with gentle nudges, while your inside leg acts as a brace to direct the impulsion forward, keeping his body erect. Nudges from the inside leg should come only if he drastically veers into the circle.

Keep these cues light! If you cue too hard, the response will be relative and the mule will most likely overreact. If your mule does not comply with your body cues, only then should you reach down and give a quick tug on the direct rein. Drop it again and allow your mule to respond. Trusting your mule to take this responsibility for himself will increase his confidence in himself and in you. When he is able to perform all of his patterns with minimal mistakes, he will begin to go "on the bit."

"On the bit" simply means that your mule is accepting the connection between your hands and his lips. It does not mean that his head is set; in fact, head sets should be a direct result of the communication between the rider's aids (seat, legs, and hands) and the mule. The head set will vary with the activity being performed by the mule while the mule's body remains supple and balanced throughout. Riders are often under the misconception that the inside rein, for instance, determines the bend of a circle. Although you want the animal to bend from head to tail, the correct bending is done between the mule's hip and shoulders. Therefore, when you are working a young or spoiled mule, it is important to keep his head straight in front of the shoulders and encourage his body to do the bending. If the mule does not follow the arc of a circle, your first impulse will be to pull on the inside rein, but this often causes the shoulders to swing outside the arc while the head and neck swing inward. The proper way to correct his balance and bend is to counterbend his head and neck to the outside long enough to bring the shoulders in, then bring the head and neck back into line with the shoulders.

It is extremely important at this point that your hands remain steady, light, and even. As you gain more balance and effectiveness in your seat and legs, your hands will be more able to remain quiet and effective. Always keep your hands directly in front of you, with your thumbs up, positioned on either side of your mule's neck, just in front of the pommel of the saddle.

Instead of pulling the reins for directional changes, modify this action with a squeeze/release action of your little fingers. The hands themselves remain basically stationary, yet flexible. If your mule is slow to respond, you may need to squeeze/release several times. Try to synchronize your squeezing as the inside foreleg comes back, and release as it goes forward. Timing and rhythm are everything here—if you squeeze as the foreleg goes forward, *your* action will inhibit the *mule's* action, producing resistance.

This begins to make more sense as the seat and legs are brought into the picture and as the situation can be perceived in terms of diagonals. Your seat and legs send the mule's body forward to the bridle, where he is received by the hands. To keep his body erect most effectively, you must send your mule forward from your inside leg to your outside hand. The inside leg squeezes to propel the corresponding leg forward. The hand on that side frees the mule to go forward with the leg as your hand on the other side checks the motion and balances the animal by receiving this energy and directing it toward suspension within the forward movement. It is within this moment of suspension that you can correctly balance each stride without resistance. If you were to nudge forward on the same side that your hand squeezes, you would restrict the forward motion, giving conflicting signals to your mule that result in confusion and resistance. When your mule is balanced, it is not necessary to squeeze the hands at all—they can remain quiet with a light contact. This, however, usually happens for only a few strides at a time, particularly in the early stages of training.

With all of these technicalities to work on, you need to vary the routines to avoid boredom and frustration. Longears are capable of a variety of activities without one interfering with another. The degree to which they perform each task is only dependent upon rider-mule communication. Properly constructed conditioning programs facilitate this success through energy-channeling exercises. These next two exercises promote freedom, relaxation, regularity, and balance in your mule and allow him to burn off some of his excess energy.

In the first exercise, put four poles on the ground spaced about four feet apart. Place these poles just off-center of your arena so that you can leave your hourglass pattern from the short side. You will ride parallel to the long side and over the poles to the next short side in a straight line. Keep the poles offset from the center, because then they will be out of your way for the hourglass pattern.

Ride the hourglass pattern as before, but occasionally leave your pattern at the short end and trot down over the poles. As you go over the poles, stand up in your stirrups, sink your weight down into your heels, lean forward, and rest your hands on either side of your mule's neck, allowing him freedom in his head and neck over the poles. Keep your eyes focused straight ahead, and keep the pressure from your legs even to send him straight forward over the poles. Always ride all the way to the rail and back into the pattern again to avoid teaching your mule to cut in, stop too soon, or run off. If your mule still hurries to the rail, stop him and back up before continuing the pattern. As your mule becomes proficient at this, gradually lengthen the distance between the poles. This promotes stretching, relaxation, and lengthening of the muscles in both the mule and rider, enhancing the quality of his gaits. It is the basis for learning to lengthen and shorten the strides of your mule at will.

In the second gymnastics exercise, position an eighteen-inch cavaletti (or a little lower) on the other side of center from your ground poles. Walk off about three of your strides (about ten to twelve feet) on either side of the cavaletti, and lay down a ground pole. Trot to the first ground pole and go over the cavaletti. Proceed to the next ground pole, then go straight to the rail. Stop and back up before doing it again. If your mule rushes the obstacle, stop him before he reaches the rail, back up, then continue on. Use the same rider form as used for over the ground poles — two-point leg position with your hands on his neck until he is over the second ground pole.

When he responds well to control over the obstacle, trot over the first ground pole and over

Meredith Hodges jumps Little Jack Horner at the Lucky Three Ranch in Loveland, Colorado, 1990. "If mules can do, then donkeys can, too!"

the cavaletti. Then canter on over the second ground pole to the rail. Again, stop your mule if necessary. When he canters and stops easily, you can begin to canter to the rail. Continue on around and do it a couple of more times before stopping.

If timing or hesitation become problems, put a ground pole on a large circle and canter your mule around and over it. As you approach the ground pole, count your mule's strides before the pole out loud—"1, 2, 3, pole." It is probably a good idea to do this exercise in both directions a few times before you go to your cavaletti and ground poles. This will help you both to get in rhythm, allow you to be aware of your mule's length of stride, and help your mule to adjust his strides accordingly. These types of exercises add a little constructive playtime to your training program.

These exercises are not exclusively for those who wish to go on to jumping. They are equine gymnastics designed to improve the condition and response of your animal. All of the exercises described in this series can be applied to horses, mules, and donkeys alike. I do find, however, that donkeys are not too fond of lunging; therefore, I generally skip that part with them. If you respect your animal's physical limitations and are patient and rewarding, you will have fun with these exercises. Be sure to take a lot of short breaks walking on the long rein so that you and your mule do not become stressed. Praise him every time he does well, and have patience when he doesn't. My own Little Jack Horner will attest to the fact that loving, learning, and leaping with longears can be a lot of fun!

Lucky Three Mae Bea C.T., stadium jumping. Stadium jumping? No problem for Meredith and Mae Bea C.T.!

Right: Lucky Three Ciji, jumping in winter.

Bitterroot Spider Dee: Place your ground poles about four feet apart. Do not be alarmed if your mule trips, stumbles, or refuses the ground poles in the beginning. It will take him a few times to figure out what they are and how to negotiate them. Working over ground poles and cavaletti will greatly enhance your mule's balance. When the mule has learned to negotiate the ground poles, he makes it look effortless. Now he is ready to move on to cavaletti.

Bitterroot Spider Dee: From your ground pole, allow your mule his head, and shift all of your weight into your heels. Encourage him forward over the raised cavaletti. Be sure to start low and work up gradually. As he goes over, be sure that your hands are well up and rested on his neck to allow him freedom of movement. If you have problems keeping your hands on his neck over the cavaletti, you may need to put a strap around his neck for you to grab.

When your mule becomes proficient at the lowest setting, he can go on to the next. Your ground poles should be set about nine feet on either side of the cavaletti to encourage your mule to jump forward instead of up into the air. At first, just trot through until he is confident. Then, you can trot to the cavaletti and encourage your mule to canter after the jump. When this goes well, he can canter all the way.

At the highest setting on the cavaletti, it is more important than ever to keep yourself organized and meticulous about your body position. Above all, keep your eyes focused well ahead to keep your mule's balance from falling on the forehand. Do the same exercises that you did before, and remember to do them in both directions to keep your mule balanced on both sides of his body. The cavaletti is set up so that it can be approached from either direction.

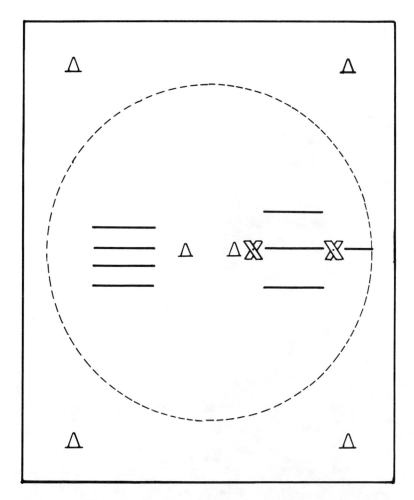

To keep shuffling ground poles and cavaletti to a minimum, use the ground pole from your cavaletti setup as a canter pole, and position your large circle in the center of your arena.

Meredith Hodges and Lucky Three Sundowner demonstrate the leg yields, showing how the distance that your mule steps laterally will increase with time and proper conditioning through exercise.

CHAPTER XXIII

Lateral Work under Saddle

It is important to develop a solid forward base before moving on to more advanced lateral work, because the young mule tends to fall laterally out of balance. The exercises discussed to this point help the mule establish a solid forward movement that causes him to engage the hindquarters and move forward into the bridle in a more balanced fashion. After working gymnastics over ground poles and cavaletti, your mule should begin to feel more balanced, and his response to your aids should become more sensitive. He should begin to take more responsibility for carrying his own body and allow you to pay closer attention to your own balance and aids. At this point you can become more serious about lateral work.

Begin your warmup through the hourglass pattern as usual, doing it in both directions before going on to the next step. Next, review first your turn on the forehand, then the lateral wheel, doing these exercises again in both directions. You now have too many different exercises to be able to review them all each time you ride; therefore, begin to focus on warming up with activities related to your training for that particular day. Vary the routine each time that you ride, because it will make the exercises more interesting for you and for your mule, and it will help to keep your mule from anticipating. For example, one day you may incorporate rider-controlled forward and reverse movement (i.e., western-pleasure and trail-related exercises), another day you may work on self-balancing forward movement (cavaletti and ground poles), and another day you may focus on lateral movement. Remember to incorporate a day of complete rest for your mule in between, because he needs time to recuperate and regroup. I usually rest my mules every other day; it seems to give them time to absorb each lesson more thoroughly and keeps them more mentally and physically willing.

In the first lateral exercise, move through the hourglass pattern, making small, ten-meter circles on each of the four corners. Make sure that you have already warmed up with your turn on the forehand and the lateral wheel. After doing the circles a couple of times, begin to ask for more. Circle your corner cone. As you come back to the pattern, follow the arc of your circle until your mule's nose is pointed directly toward the center cone situated farthest from you (i.e., you have two center cones; doing a right-leg yield off of the left leg, point his nose to the center cone farthest to the right). When his body is straight on the diagonal from corner cone to center cone, sit briefly for your half-halt (causing a slight hesitation in your mule). Do a thirty-four-degree turn on the forehand from your outside leg, and bring the mule's hindquarters parallel to the long side of the arena. Keeping your body erect, nudge your mule laterally and forward to the center. Then resume your pattern to the second corner and repeat the exercise.

It is important that your mule remain straight for this exercise; therefore, don't pull so much on the reins that you cock his head one way or the other. Using draw reins can help stabilize the front and reduce resistance in your mule for these exercises. Attach them between the front legs, through the snaffle rings, then back to your saddle at the girth rings. When you leg-yield to the right, your right rein will be your leading and supportive rein; your left rein will be your direct rein, inviting your mule to look ever so slightly to the left (just enough so that you can see his eyeball, but no more!). Do not allow his body to bend. Your right leg is passive behind the girth, supporting your mule and controlling the hindquarters both sideways and forward in a push-relax fashion. Coordinate your push and relax with your mule's stride. As you push-relax with your left leg, integrate your squeeze-release on the reins. The squeeze-release on the right rein should be a little firmer than that from the left rein, because the left rein is your direct rein and should be held almost steady to maintain proper body carriage. As you push with your leg, squeeze with your opposite hand. When you relax this leg, release the rein. The push-squeezing occurs as the mule's right front leg comes back toward you and the right hind leg steps forward.

Keep your movements small and definite. Think of your own right shoulder leading to the cone, but do not allow your right hand to stray too far to the right of your mule's neck or allow your body to lean too far to the left. This will

Little Jack Horner — English.

speed up your mule's shoulders and get them too far ahead of his haunches in the leg yield.

Try to stay as relaxed as you can during this exercise—the most common problem among riders is trying to do too much to get this lateral response. Give your cues and allow your mule to respond. Be content with one or two good leg-yield steps in the beginning. It won't be more than a few weeks before he understands this new concept. Using the draw reins should help keep him soft in your hands, but don't fret if his nose stretches out a little in the beginning—this is generally just a reaction of intense concentration for the young mule, and he will relax as he better understands your intent.

The next exercise is a variation on the first one, except instead of yielding from corner to center, you yield from center to corner. Make a ten-meter circle when you reach the center cones, then yield to the corner opposite your inside leg. In other words, make a ten-meter circle to the left, then yield from the left leg to the corner cone on your right. Continue through your pattern back to center, then circle to the right and leg-yield to the left. Do this a few times in each direction of the pattern. This helps your mule to realize that leg yields can be done from more places than just corners, and it causes him to place more value on your aids.

If your mule has difficulty with the lateral movement within the pattern, the next exercise will help him to better understand the aids. Position your mule at a forty-five-degree angle to the long side of your arena, with his haunches in toward the center and his face to the rail. Ask him for a few steps of leg yield; the same aids apply. If you are going right, the left leg and right rein are active and are push-squeezing while your left rein and right leg are passive and supportive. When your mule complies with a few steps of leg yield, move his shoulders back in front of his haunches, and continue straight forward, praising him lavishly!

Lateral work is difficult, because both you and your mule are searching for balance from stride to stride. The best advice is, *don't try too hard!* Do what is outlined here, and allow the movement to happen. Do not try to control the movement itself. Direct your mule with the proper cues, and let him control his own body in compliance with your commands. The most common mistake is to shift your own body around too much, which hinders and restricts the response of your mule. Do your job in cueing and maintaining your own balance, and let your mule do his job.

Lateral work is so stressful that it is best to work on it only once or twice a week, and *never* two days in a row! If you do, you run the risk of confusing your mule and interfering with his forward movement. Lateral movement becomes much easier relatively quickly if you just take your time, relax, and enjoy.

All of the exercises that your mule does will help facilitate good balance, rhythm, and submission to the aids.

Lucky Three Ciji: Doing the leg yield on the rail under saddle is not much different from the ground-driving, except that you give your mule a quick nudge with your leg as you pull (or squeeze) your leading rein.

If your mule gets a little fast, or ahead with his shoulders, just stop, straighten, and begin again. Pull . . . release, pull . . . release; nudge . . . hold, nudge . . . hold; one . . . step . . . at . . . a . . . time! Practice these exercises until your mule moves laterally easily and with only as many steps as you desire.

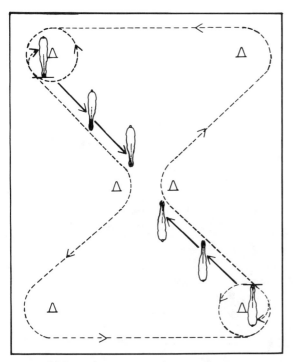

Leg yield from the corner to the center.

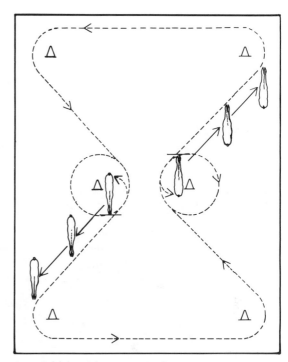

Leg yield from the center to the corner.

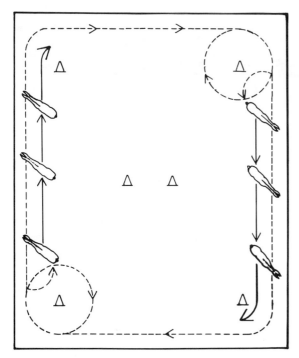

Leg yield down the long side.

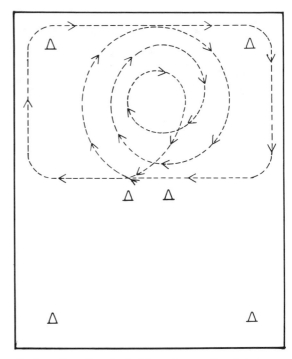

Begin on the rail, and spiral down to a smaller circle in three revolutions. Then leg-yield back to the larger circle.

When you train for good equine posture with balance, rhythm, and submission, English or Western, the result should be the same.

CHAPTER XXIV

Better Balance and Lateral Response

By this time, those of you who generally ride Western are probably asking why I haven't progressed to sliding stops and turn-arounds. The answer is simple. Although your mule is probably capable of assimilating such movements, as he does when he is playing, his understanding of the aids is still limited, and his muscular development is still not adequate for the stress placed upon him by these movements. If you start too soon on these maneuvers, you run the risk of muscular strain, bowed tendons, or worse. It is always difficult to watch someone else spinning and sliding his young mule, and maybe even winning in events that require these movements, but if you are to maximize the "use-life" of your mule, it only makes sense to condition him slowly and methodically to minimize stress and strain—both mental and physical. After all, a ballet dancer does not become a prima ballerina overnight. It takes years for all factors to be meshed together in a beautiful picture of fluidity and harmony.

It is unfortunate that plain common sense is often forfeited for short-term monetary gain and recognition. I have spoken to many reputable trainers who wish that their clients would give them more time to train the animals so that the animals would not be stressed, but the story is always the same. People are always gung-ho to go out and win at the time that they are mentally geared up to do so, with little or no regard for the animal's health and welfare. They are unwilling to contribute the financial expense of long-term training. In Europe, where the equestrian arts are an important part of the culture, you find far less of this kind of abuse; there is more respect for the art, and thus for the animals. The United States Dressage Federation is growing rapidly in this country as equestrians are beginning to respect the European attitudes and to realize the true importance of their own attitudes toward training.

But enough philosophical talk—let's get on with the training. The exercises already described should help your mule begin to understand the concept and function of your legs as being more than an impulsive device. Your legs direct him both forward and laterally. As he begins to understand this better, he will speed up less and less when your legs are "on." He will begin to listen to the "direction" of your legs.

You have taken your mule through balanced circles and moved him laterally from those circles onto diagonals. Next, you need to teach him how to move laterally on the circle. This will enable him to reduce and enlarge circles with a simple response to your aids.

Start by laterally enlarging the circle. Begin at the walk on a twenty-meter (approximately sixty-foot) circle. Spiral down to as small a circle as your mule is comfortable with, but do not allow him to fall out of frame (i.e., lean in). Do this in about three revolutions. When he successfully completes one or two revolutions of the smallest circle, leg-yield him back to the largest circle, skipping the revolutions in between. Use the aids previously discussed. If you are leg-yielding to the right, your right rein is your leading and supportive rein. Your left rein is your direct rein, inviting your mule to look ever-so-slightly to the left. Your right leg is passive, behind the girth, supporting your mule and controlling his hindquarters. Your left leg is active in a rhythmic, nudging fashion.

Meredith and Lucky Three Sundowner wait patiently for their results at the Clearview Farm Dressage Schooling Show in spring 1990.

Do this exercise at the walk, the trot, and the canter in both directions of the circle, but do not proceed to a faster gait until you feel that your mule understands the implications of your aids. Be sure to use your half-halts to balance him with every stride. This keeps him smooth and confident. Be sure to praise him for each successful completion of this pattern.

Cindy Powell and Lucky Three Stardust over poles at a mule show in Virginia.

Allow him to walk on the long rein, relax, and catch his breath after one or two completions of this pattern at the trot and canter before repeating it, because this pattern is taxing for a young mule. This will prevent fatigue and frustration for both of you. Pay special attention to your own body position and see that you remain upright, with correct posture, particularly at the faster gaits. Any shifting of your own balance either backward, forward, or laterally will interfere with your mule's ability to perform correctly and may cause him to lose his balance, become fearful, and act resistant.

When your mule begins to understand the aids for the leg yield, teaching him to side pass is a cinch. Begin by placing a pole on the ground about five feet from the rail and lying parallel to it. Position your mule with his nose to the rail and his front quarters between the rail and the pole. His hindquarters should be on the other side of the pole so that he stands over it. Give the aids to leg yield in the direction that you desire, nudging with your active leg and leading with the opposite rein. If he becomes confused and moves from side to side, just move the front quarters one step in the right direction, then move the hindquarters in behind as if you were going to do a turn-on-the-forehand. The rail will keep him from going forward, and if you are patient, he will soon learn that you wish to go sideways. "Feel" the amount of tension that you need on the reins to accomplish this maneuver. Then, when he is reacting easily, move the pole to the middle of the arena and repeat the exercise until he is responding freely and easily.

A variation on this theme is side passing the "T." Position three poles on the ground in the shape of a "T," allowing enough space at the junction for your mule to pass his feet through easily while keeping the pole directly beneath his barrel (about twenty-four to twenty-eight inches apart). Begin at the top of the "T," at the outside end of the pole. Your mule's head should face the top of the "T" and straddle the pole. Then side pass to the center. Keeping your legs and his hindquarters steady, use your hands to do a one-quarter turn-on-the-haunches, moving the forequarters through the space provided and into position to side pass down the leg of the "T." Stop, then side pass back to the top of the "T." At the top of the "T," do a turn-on-the-forehand, bringing your mule's hindquarters through the space provided to the top of the "T" so that he is straddling the next pole and is facing the leg of the "T." Complete the side pass of the third and final pole.

Exercises like these in the side pass facilitate control over each step that your mule takes. They can be done even if your mule isn't up to hard work that day. Be slow and meticulous, and you will soon find that such exercises are relaxing and enormously productive.

Tea Party as a three-year-old, show by Diane Hunter-McElvain.

Lucky Three Sundowner in a canter spiral.

In order to do the canter spiral down to the trot, your mule must be cantering in an uphill balance. If his balance is not shifted backward, he will not be able to turn.

Whether you begin on the right or the left, the sequence is the same: Follow the top of the "T" to the center, do a turn-on-the-haunches, and proceed down the leg of the "T." Then, side pass back up the leg of the "T," do a turn-on-the-forehand, and complete the side pass across the top of the "T."

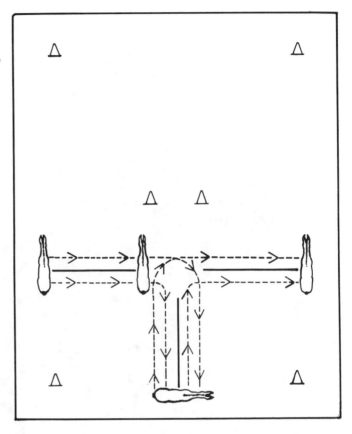

Lucky Three Ciji: side passing the "T."

Meredith Hodges and Lucky Three Mae Bea C.T., Utah State Fair, 1989, English Pleasure.

CHAPTER XXV

Clarifying the Forward/Lateral Connection

It is important that you properly condition your young mule with a carefully sequenced program of gymnastics exercises so that his mind and body develop correctly. Spending time cultivating a smooth, fluid forward motion with rhythm and cadence will help your mule achieve this goal and will enable him to perform more difficult movements more easily. Work over ground poles and cavaletti helps build muscle, particularly in the hindquarters, and this will help your mule carry your weight more easily through lateral movements, stops, and lengthenings. Your mule will become less resistant and frustrated, and this will be apparent in his tail carriage.

You may notice that after you introduce a few simple lateral movements, your mule's forward motion becomes a little shaky again. It is now time to clarify the connection between forward motion and lateral motion. With his increased understanding of your seat and legs, this should be a fairly simple process through a few simple exercises.

Ask your mule to walk a twenty-meter (approximately sixty feet) circle, maintaining rhythm, cadence, proper flexion, and bend. Then, in rhythm, change your aids to a slight counterbend, and ask for a turn-on-the-forehand, sending his haunches in toward the center of the circle until he is reversed. At the precise instant that he is in position to start following the circle in the opposite direction, release your pressure on the reins and send him forward again on the new circle. You will need to hold him back a little with the reins through the turn-on-the-forehand to keep him from "swapping ends" through the turn, but to maintain the forward motion, you must release your pressure at the instant he completes the turn!

Do *not* hold back on the reins with steady pressure during the turn-on-the-forehand. Rather, complete the turn with a series of half-halts with your seat and with a squeeze/release action on the reins. If you do this, your final release will come as a natural sequence to the turn, and it will be in rhythm and harmony with your mule. You can do this exercise at the walk, trot, and canter, slowing to the walk each time for the turn-on-the-forehand.

Next, you need to cultivate the turn-on-the-haunches. Your mule's lateral work on the T-poles will have given him a little understanding of what this is all about. Again, walk him on a twenty-meter circle. Then, when you are ready to make the turn, nudge him rhythmically and hard with your outside leg. Keep your weight centered over his body with a passive inside leg, and maintain contact with your outside rein so that his head remains straight. Lead him to the new direction with a squeeze/release action on your inside rein. Be careful not to inhibit the forward motion! It is better that he do small circles to complete the turn than fall back over his haunches.

As in the turn-on-the-forehand, nudge and give, squeeze and release; a mule will lean hard against continuous pressure. Keep practicing this exercise, maintaining his body between your aids. When he does well at the walk, move on to the trot and canter, slowing to the walk for the turn. And even if your mule makes a mistake, praise him for his effort and go on. This will make him a much more cooperative partner, and eventually you will succeed at what you have set out to accomplish!

Once your mule figures out his footwork through these turns and has had the chance to build up his body physically, you can think about increasing your demand for speed and finesse. This comes much later, however. To attempt any more than this right now most likely will destroy his forward motion, cadence, and rhythm and will cause much frustration and fatigue.

"Fencing" a mule is an excellent exercise for improving the quality of the turn-on-the-haunches for reining and cow work, but because of the sensitive nature of the mule and his slow physical maturation, it usually causes too much stress and frustration if attempted too early. The mule may even perform well for a couple of years after this quicker training, but before long, he may sour on the movements, anticipate, and possibly even begin to run off with you to avoid doing them. Better to take it slow and easy and maintain your rapport and under-

standing with him. After all, mules generally live a lot longer than horses—so why get impatient and try to do too much too soon? Wouldn't you rather have a long-lasting and pleasant relationship with a mule that is happy with his work?

Backing is something that I generally do in-between the exercises from the time I begin to ride the mule. I usually don't put too much emphasis on the actual quality of the back until now, however, when my mule has a firmer understanding of what it means to go forward. Correct backing, after all, is initiated through forward motion. Your mule must be sensitive to your aids to understand this concept.

When teaching a young mule to back up straight and true, start by asking him to take one step forward. Then lean slightly forward with your upper body, squeeze the rein, and nudge with your leg on the same side as the forward leg of your mule. When that front leg comes back, squeeze and nudge on the other side. Keep alternating sides for as many strides as you desire to back up. Be sure to be contented with just a step or two at first, and build on that with each new practice session. Praise your mule lavishly for successes, and stroke him gently and calmly if he makes a mistake.

During the backing procedure, you should get the sensation that your seat and legs are, in fact, walking backward with your mule, even though your upper body is shifted slightly forward. By bending your upper body forward, you lighten your seat and allow your mule to move in under your weight. When you wish him to stop, simply sit up straight and drop your weight back down into the saddle. With careful practice, you will be able to move your mule backward exactly as many steps as you desire and communicate with him clearly and concisely.

If you follow the guidelines described here, there will soon be no trail obstacle or class too difficult. The secret is in the balance, the harmony, and the communication between you and your mule.

Assuming that you have followed all of the training exercises described previously, you should now be seeing some obvious results. Your mule should be carrying his own body in balance for longer periods of time with fewer corrections, his response to your aids should be more prompt and correct, and he should take your corrections with much less fear and apprehension. The rides that you get on him should be smooth, steady, rhythmic, and swinging, because he has become more steady and balanced—and so have you! His longer periods of maintained balance should give you the opportunity to feel the power and thrust of the hindquarters more clearly through your seat and legs.

He should now be getting less and less "behind" your legs; your legs push him forward easily as you receive him gently, yet firmly, into your hands. To identify this feeling, walk the perimeter of your arena. Alternate your leg pressure against your mule's body as his outside front leg comes back to you. At the same time, release on the rein of the front leg going forward—but only ever so slightly. If he is not stepping smartly forward, bend your knees a little more so that your calves connect on the swell of his barrel. Now, nudge him again; he should step forward easily. The energy that you feel should seem like he is almost "shooting forward out from underneath your seat." If you are soft, yet firm and receiving, in your hands, he should not shoot forward and out of control, but should round his body vertically with good hindquarter engagement and lightness in his body. If your mule still gets a little heavy in your hands, squeeze and release your hands and legs, just slightly alternating your rein pressure, until he submits and rounds.

A very simple exercise can help your mule learn more about the meaning of your aids— your seat, your hands, and your legs. As you walk him down the long side of your arena, count out loud, "One . . . and . . . two . . . and . . . three . . . and . . . four . . ." and repeat. Do this in unison with each of his steps, and try to maintain his best active, yet natural, rhythm. If he breaks this rhythm with a trip or a misstep, no matter— keep counting on in rhythm and encourage him with your aids to get back on track.

Do the long side of your arena with longer reins; with each step, encourage him to stretch down into the bridle. Alternate your legs and hands, and allow your arms to extend a little with each step forward. Before you turn the

corner at the end of the long side of your arena, change your aids so that you begin to check, then follow, with both reins at the same time (shortening the reins with each step). As you check, squeeze with both legs simultaneously. Change your verbal rhythmic count to, "Two . . . and . . . two . . . and . . . two . . ." and so on. Be sure that your legs are positioned securely on the swell of his barrel. Your mule should then begin to collect his walk on the short side of the arena by stepping under with the hindquarters and rounding his body vertically. Hold him and rebalance him with every stride, especially around the corners. Once he reaches the next long side, change your aids back to alternate pressure and count again, "One . . . and . . . two . . . and . . . three . . . and . . . four . . . and . . . ," and encourage him to lengthen his frame again and stretch down into the bridle.

This exercise will clarify the meaning of your aids to your mule in even finer detail and will help him to become much more responsive to your aids. You can use this exercise as a starter warmup and anytime during your workout when you are walking and resting. This should *not* be a stressful exercise. As your mule becomes lighter in the bridle when you ask him to collect himself, you can do this same exercise at the trot and canter. When you ask your mule to collect himself, you want him to round forward into the bridle from your legs. Avoid contact with your hands that causes him to merely drop his head or suck back into collection. *When* you ask with your aids is very important. You do not want to cause him to fall off balance so that you must time your squeezes: in the trot and walk when the outside front leg comes back; and in the canter when he is in suspension or when the front legs are coming back to you. In order for him to be truly "on the bit," he must round his body from back to front vertically and maintain active forward motion with attention to lateral bend around corners.

Another exercise that will help your mule to stay "on the bit" for longer periods requires you to rearrange your arena "furniture," or cones. Place your "gates" of cones on the quarter line spaced evenly along the long side of your arena. Two cones make one "gate." You can set this up along both long sides on the quarter lines if you have enough cones; eight cones are needed for each line of "gates."

Begin your exercise at the walk. Walk through the first "gate" and stop between the cones at the second "gate." Wait about fifteen seconds, then proceed through the third "gate." Circle to the nearest rail, coming back through the third "gate' twice (about a ten-meter circle), then go on to the fourth "gate" and halt. If cones are placed on both sides of the arena, continue on around the short side of your arena and repeat down the next long side. If not, continue through the short side and lengthen your mule's gait down the long side as described in the first exercise. When you come to the long side with the "gates," just turn up the quarter line and proceed through the "gates." Even if you have cones on both sides, it is advisable to allow your animal to lengthen from time to time just to keep him relaxed, supple, and responsive. Although it seems simple enough, work in collection can be taxing. It is important to give your mule frequent rests between attempts.

As you go through the cones, be sure to feel your mule going in front of your legs. Keep your own balance upright and straight, and feel the different pressure in your seat as you move along, as you halt, and as you circle. You are trying to get your mule to pay closer attention to your seat as you lighten your rein and leg aids. As you are moving along, your pelvis will rock forward and backward, stretching your abdominal muscles and flexing your lower back. When you come to a halt, you should deliberately slow this action by stiffening your lower back and sitting down on your seatbones.

At first, your mule will probably lean on the reins and take a few steps through the halt. As you practice more, however, you will find that he learns the pattern and begins to stop as you begin to ask more and more with your seat and use your hands and legs for balance. You will know that he is working this exercise correctly when his halts become consistently square and you are able to remain upright throughout the transition.

What you are trying to achieve with these two exercises is to develop a better understand-

Meredith Hodges and Lucky Three Firestorm, Utah State Fair, 1989, Green English Pleasure.

ing between you and your mule concerning the concept of the half-halt. The purpose of the half-halt is to allow you to check and balance your mule's body at any given time. It takes a long time to reach the goal of riding and balancing every stride, but this is what you are striving for constantly.

In the beginning, your mule may not let you check and balance him easily. With practice, however, he will begin to realize that you mean him no harm, and he will be better able to trust you and submit to your aids. Good posture and good balance feel good; it doesn't take a mule too long to realize that your aids are for his benefit and comfort. He will be more willing to let you control him more with each new lesson. The final outcome is that you will be able to control every step of every gait so that your mule remains in good balance. As a result, he will be in good condition and ready to do anything that you might want to do. This is what a "finished mule" is all about.

Make sure that the first step your mule takes is forward!

Keep your hands even and his head and neck in a straight line at first.

Lead him in the direction that you wish with your rein while you keep the other rein steady and in line. Nudge him with your leg just behind the girth, and hold steady with the other leg.

If he gets a little resistant, stop and take the time to relax and round him back into frame. Soon he will learn to relax and stay round throughout the turn.

Gary and Meredith Hodges with Lucky Three Eclipse, National Western Stock Show Grand Champion Model Mule.

CHAPTER XXVI

Enhancing Strength and Muscular Development

Your mule learns many new things during his basic training. In his very early years, he learns to establish a working relationship with humans. Exposure to humans at an early age thwarts any fear that he might have as long as his exposure is a positive experience. In showmanship training and lunging, he learns verbal and physical languages to enhance his communication with humans. And through his series of gymnastics exercises, he is introduced to our aids. Thus, his forward movement is enhanced through the gaits with rhythm, cadence, and balance.

He then gains a useful lateral response. The use of "halt-halts" enables you to command the attention of your mule so that he can prepare for any changes that might be asked of him. The final task in basic training is to call the mule's attention to his vertical balance and the part that it plays in speed and control and more complicated maneuvers. Thus, it is time to introduce the shoulder-in, the lengthened trot, and the lengthened canter.

To perform the shoulder-in properly, it is important to understand its purpose. It causes the mule to engage his hindquarters so that they carry the bulk of his weight. This gives him more freedom and suppleness in his shoulders and front quarters. A strong base must be established to carry this weight forward while the shoulders, light and free, proceed forward laterally.

The shoulder-in is done on a straight line. Normally, an animal traveling in a straight line makes two tracks in the dirt behind him, because the front legs are positioned directly in front of the back legs. In the shoulder-in, the shoulders are positioned so that they cause a three-track pattern behind—the inside front foot makes one track, the outside front foot and the inside hind foot make one track, and the outside hind foot makes one track.

Begin walking the perimeter of your arena. When you reach the corner before the long side, make a ten-meter circle. As you close your circle at the start of the long side of your arena, maintain the bend that you had for the circle with steady pressure on your inside rein. At the same time, nudge your mule with alternate leg pressure in synchronization with his hind legs as they each go forward. Squeeze your outside rein at the same time that you squeeze with your outside leg, then release the outside rein. Ride the hindquarters straight forward with your seat and legs as you offset the shoulders with your hands. Be careful that your inside rein is not so tight that your mule bends only his neck to the inside. As you squeeze with the outside aids, feel your mule rock his balance back to the hindquarters, giving you the sensation of pedaling backward on a bicycle. At this same time, you should feel the front quarters begin to lighten and become supple.

Take your time and don't try too hard! At first, be content with a couple of steps of shoulder-in. Then immediately swing your mule's shoulders back to the track, and send him straight forward with more energy. Slow your mule's gait through the short side of the arena, then repeat the exercise on the next long side. As your mule begins to understand the concept of rocking his balance to the hindquarters, the surge of energy that you feel when he straightens will become more and more powerful.

Much body coordination is involved in this exercise, and at first, you may feel like you are all thumbs. Time, patience, and practice will bring about positive results, so stay with it! Over time, do this exercise at the walk, the trot, and the canter, and go both ways in the arena. Don't forget to praise your mule for each correct step that he gives you!

The next exercise to enhance hindquarter engagement and lengthen the stride is quite simple, yet still a little tricky. Track the perimeter of your arena again. This time, collect the trot on the short sides, then urge your mule on down the long sides. To add variation, urge him to lengthen across the diagonals (from corner to corner) as well. Your mule's first impulse probably will be to shift his weight to the forehand and speed up. For this reason, do not push him too hard too soon. At first, just ask for a little more energy; be aware that your rhythm and cadence are not lost as his stride increases. Keep the forehand light and free while you ride the hindquarters. Let your hand open slightly, with the foreleg going forward on the same side, and close as the leg comes back. This will help you to determine how far you can let that stride go before the balance begins to shift forward. It also will allow you to check the balance with your hands before it begins to shift.

Lucky Three Ciji, Western pleasure. Whether riding Western or English, the best posture for your animal to perform is basically the same.

As your mule gains strength in the hindquarters and is better able to carry your weight, his lengthenings will continue to improve until, perhaps a year or so later, he will be able to fully extend his stride. This exercise can be done at both the trot and canter. I caution you, however, that if your mule begins to rush, ask for less.

Another exercise that is helpful in lengthening the trot is to canter your mule around the arena, then cross half of your diagonal at the canter. Break to the trot and finish the diagonal. After the diagonal, sit the trot through the short side of your arena, pick up the canter on the long side again, then cross the next available diagonal again and repeat the pattern. The drive that a mule gets from his hindquarters in the canter will carry through into the trot for the few strides on the diagonal and will create the true lengthening. This is your opportunity to tell your mule, "Yes, yes, this is what I want when I squeeze you on!"

Learning to ride from back to front (from the hindquarters) will greatly improve the harmony between you and your mule. Loss of balance seems to be the single most common cause of problems in riding animals. Carrying your weight and his over the strongest part of your mule's body minimizes the chance for a loss of balance, and recovery from such a loss is easier. Your mule will soon discover that your aids are indeed for his benefit as well as for your own, and he will become more accepting of them over time. As he becomes more balanced, you will find a world of different activities that you and your mule can do!

Lucky Three Sundowner at a working trot.

Meredith Hodges and Lucky Three Sundowner practice shoulder-in left.

Meredith Hodges and Lucky Three Sundowner practice shoulder-in right.

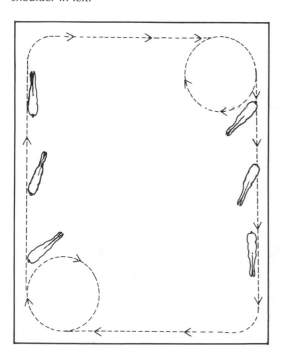

Shoulder-in.

Lucky Three Sundowner: Lengthening the trot requires that the mule maintain the same rhythm while increasing the distance covered. This does not mean to go faster. In order to lengthen the trot effectively, the mule's shoulders must be elevated. For this reason, you may have to raise your hands a little and sit back.

Lengthen the stride on the long side and across the diagonal.

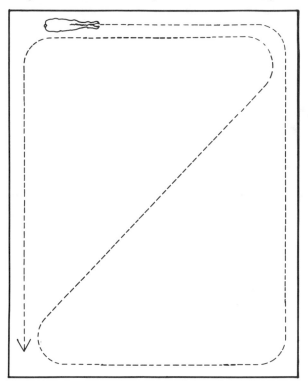

Change of rein across the diagonal (simple change).

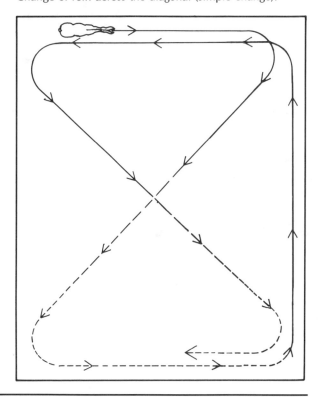

Diane Hunter-McElvain and Tea Party, Western Pleasure.

CHAPTER XXVII

Fine Tuning the Rider

No training series would be complete without examining the principles and philosophy behind training techniques. My philosophy is based on the principle that I am not, in fact, training donkeys and mules. Rather, I am cultivating relationships with them by assigning meaning to my body language that they can understand.

My own level of understanding changes and grows over time; therefore, I must assume that my animals' understanding grows, too, and I must gauge my explanations accordingly. In the beginning, the emotional needs of the young mule are different from those of an older animal. The young mule needs to overcome many instincts that would protect him in the wild but that are inappropriate in a domestic situation. In this case, the focus must be on developing friendship and confidence in the young mule while establishing my own dominance in a nonthreatening manner. This is accomplished through a lot of positive reinforcement in the beginning, including gentle touches, a reassuring voice, and lots of treats. Expressions of disapproval should be kept at a minimum.

As the mule grows with me, he will realize that I do not wish to harm him. Next he will develop a rather pushy attitude in an attempt to assert his own dominance, because he is now confident that this behavior is acceptable. When this occurs, I reevaluate my reward system and save excessive praise for the new exercises as he learns them. I allow the learned behavior to be treated as the norm, and I praise it more passively, yet in an appreciative manner. This is the delicate concept of give and take in a relationship from an emotional standpoint. As in any good relationship, I am polite and considerate of my mules and donkeys. After all, "You can catch more flies with sugar than you can with vinegar!"

Many details of both mule and trainer must also be considered from a physical standpoint. In the beginning, unless you are a professional trainer with years of proper schooling, you are not likely to be the most balanced and coordinated of riders, and you may lack absolute control over your body language. By the same token, the untrained mule will be lacking in the muscular coordination and strength to respond to your intent of performing certain movements. For these reasons, you must modify your approaches to fit each new situation and modify again to perfect it, keeping in mind that your main goal is to establish a good relationship with your mule and *not* just to train him! It is up to you, the trainer, to decide the cause of any resistance and to modify techniques that will temper that resistance, be it mental or physical.

For instance, I have a three-year-old mule that is learning to lunge without the benefit of the round pen. The problem is that he refuses to go around me more than a couple of times without running off. I first need to assess the situation by brainstorming all the probable reasons why he might keep doing such an annoying thing. Is he frightened? Is he bored? Is he mischievous? Has he been calm and accepting of most things until now? And, most important, is my own body language causing this to occur?

Animals are all different, as are humans, and each learns in his own way, as do humans. Once in a while, you will meet a mule that cannot learn in the conventional sequence of events. He perceives a situation just differently enough to make it extremely difficult. In the case of the mule that will not lunge independently on the line, I found that he needs additional learning aids. I may either need to put a round pen around him to "force" him to comply, or I may wait until he is broke to saddle before I try to lunge him again with just the line. I have worked with many mules that wouldn't lunge at first, but they would ground-drive and accept a saddle and rider with no problem. After this, they seemed to lunge quite easily! Learn to be fair and flexible in your approach to problems. Be firm in your own convictions, but be sensitive to situations that can change, and be willing to make those changes as the occasion arises.

Just as mental changes occur, so do physical changes. As muscles develop and coordination improves, you will need to do less and less to cause certain movements. For example, in the case of the leg yield, you may have to turn your mule's head a little in the

Diane Hunter-McElvain pole bending on the "great" mule, Dr. Feelgood, Texas State Fair, 1979.

opposite direction to get him to step sideways and forward. As he becomes stronger, more coordinated, and understands your aids, you can then begin to straighten his body more and work your own body less. Granted, you began by doing things the "wrong" way, yet you put your mule "on the road" to the right way. You assimilated an action in response to your leg that can now be perfected over time. In essence, you have simply said, "First you learn to move away from my leg, then you can learn to do it gracefully!"

The same concept works in the case of the trainer or the rider. Sometimes you must do things that are not quite right in the beginning to get your own body to assimilate correctness. As I said, we all perceive things a little differently, and our perception depends on how we are introduced to something and on whether or not we can understand or perform it.

It is nearly impossible for the inexperienced horseman to perceive and control unused seat bones as a viable means of controlling the mule. Reins and legs are much more prevalent. In order to help such a rider perceive the seat bones more clearly, it sometimes helps to start by involving the whole lower body. Earlier, I suggested that you pedal forward in conjunction with the front legs to begin facilitating this action. Connecting this action with the front legs of the mule allows you to "see" something concrete with which you can coordinate, plus the pedaling encourages necessary independent movement in the seat bones from side to side and forward. When you begin to "feel" this sensation, you can begin to rationalize that when the foreleg comes back, the corresponding hind leg is coming forward, and that is what your seat bone is actually corresponding with. When you perceive this, mentally and physically, you can begin to pedal backward, putting you even closer in synchronization with your mule's body. As your leg muscles become more stable, actual movement becomes less, more emphasis is directed toward your center

of gravity, and more responsibility is placed on your seat bones. Using this approach, muscles are put into use and coordinated through gymnastics exercises that eventually lead to correct position and effective cueing.

Achieving balance and harmony with your mule requires more than just balancing and conditioning your mule's body. As you begin to finish-train your mule, you need to shift your awareness more toward your own body. Your mule should already be moving fairly steadily forward in a longer frame and be basically obedient to your aids. The object in finish-training is to build the muscles in your own body so that your aids become more clearly defined and effective. This involves shedding old habits and building new ones. This takes a lot of time and should not be approached impatiently. There are no shortcuts! In order to stabilize your hands and upper body, you need to establish a firm base in your seat and legs. Ideally, you should be able to drop a plumb line from your shoulder down through your hips, through your heels, and to the ground. To maintain this plumb

Meredith Hodges and Lucky Three Mae Bea C.T. jump bridleless at the Lucky Three Ranch.

Little Jack Horner, traveling rhythmically and in a balanced fashion at a canter.

line, work to make your joints and muscles in your body more supple and flexible by using them correctly.

As you ride your mule through the walking exercise, try to stay soft, relaxed, and forward in your inner thighs and seat bones. Get the sensation that your legs are cut off at the knees, and let your seat bones walk along with your mule, lightly and in rhythm with him. If he slows down, just bend your knees and bump him alternately with your legs below the knees while you keep your seat and upper legs stable and moving forward. When collecting the walk on the short side, just bend both knees at the same time, bumping your mule simultaneously on both sides while you squeeze the reins at the same time.

In order to help you stay over the middle of your mule's back on the large circle, keep your eyes up and ahead. Shift your weight slightly to the outside stirrup, and feel it pull your inside leg snugly against your mule. Be sure that your outside leg stays in close to his barrel as you do this. On straight lines, keep your legs even, but on the arc, look a little to the outside of the circle. This will bring your inside seat bone slightly forward, allowing your legs to be in the correct position for the circle. This is partic-

ularly helpful during canter transitions.

Most people feel that they do not balance on the reins as much as they actually do. If you balance on the reins at all, your mule will be unable to achieve proper hindquarter engagement and ultimate balance. To help shift the weight from the hands and upper body to the seat and legs, you can do a simple exercise.

Put your mule on the rail at a good working walk. On the long side, drop your reins on his neck, and feel your lower body connection with him as you move along. You will need to tip your pelvis forward and stretch your abdominal muscles with each step in order to maintain your shoulder with his hip plumb line. If your lower leg remains in the correct position, your thigh muscles will be stretched on the front of your leg from your hip to your knee. There is also a slight side-to-side motion as your mule moves forward that will cause your seat bones to move independently and alternately forward. There is no doubt that you can probably do this fairly easily right from the start, but to maintain this rhythm and body position without thinking about it takes time and repetition.

When you are fairly comfortable at the walk, you can add some variation at the trot. Begin at the posting trot on the rail. When your mule is going around in a fairly steady fashion, drop your reins on his neck and continue to post. As you post down the long side, keep your upper body erect and your pelvis rocking forward from your knee. Your knee should be bent so that your legs are positioned on the barrel of your mule. Raise your arms out in front of you, parallel to your shoulders. If your mule drifts away from the rail, you need to post with a little more weight in your outside stirrup. As you go around corners, be sure to turn your eyes a little to the outside of the circle to help your position. As you approach the short side of the arena, bring your arms back, straight out from your shoulders, and keep your upper body erect. As you go through the corners, just rotate your arms and upper body slightly toward the outside of your circle. When you come to the next long side, bring your arms, once again, in front of and parallel to your shoulders, and repeat the exercise.

Notice the different pressure on your seat bones as you change your arm position. The forward arms will somewhat lighten your seat, while your arms to the side tend to exert a little more pressure. Consequently, you can send your mule more forward with your seat as you go down the long sides. You can shorten that stride with a little added pressure from the seat bones on the short sides. When you wish to halt, put your arms behind you at the small of your back to support an erect upper body, and let your weight drop down through your seat bones and legs. Remember to use your verbal commands, especially in the beginning, to clarify your aids to your mule. If your mule doesn't stop, just reach down and give a gentle tug on the reins until he stops. Before long, he will begin to make the connection between your seat and your command to "Whoa," and your seat will take precedence over your reins.

When you and your mule have become adept at the walk and the trot, add the canter. At the canter, however, keep your arms out to the side and rotate them in small circles in rhythm with the canter. Be sure to sit back and allow only your pelvis, your seat, and your thighs to stretch forward with the canter stride. Keep your upper

Gail Altieri and Ole King Jole.

body erect and your lower leg stable from the knee down. Once your mule has learned to differentiate seat and leg aids in each gait and through the transitions on the large circle, you can begin to work on directional changes through the cones.

As you practice these exercises, you will soon discover how even the slightest shift of balance can affect your mule's performance. By riding without your reins and making the necessary adjustments in your body, you will begin to condition your own muscles to work in harmony with those of your mule. As your muscles get stronger and more responsive, you will cultivate more harmony and balance with your mule. As you learn to ride more "by the seat of your pants," you will encounter less resistance in your mule, because most resistance is initiated by "bad hands." As you learn to vary the pressure in your seat accordingly, you will also encounter less resistance in your mule through his back. The stability in your lower leg also will give him a clearer path to follow between your aids.

PRO PHOTO
Pam Olsen

Meredith and Dena Hodges have exhibited Lucky Three Ciji and Mae Bea C.T. at several notable events.

CHAPTER XXVIII

Fine Tuning the Aids

As you attempted the exercises in balance by riding without the aid of your reins, you probably discovered a lot more shifting of your own balance than you imagined. This nearly imperceptible shift of balance, however, can grossly affect the balance of your mule. Until now, I have always given you a visual point of reference by allowing you to glance down at the outside front leg. Now you want to be more inwardly conscious of your own body position.

You need to repeat many of the old exercises to cultivate this kind of sensitivity. This time, close your eyes for brief periods to get the "feel" of each movement in your own body. Do not simply allow your mule to travel freely in any direction, because this will not give you an accurate feeling for any specific task. You must plan your course of action. If, for instance, you set your mule up to bend through and impulse out of the corner, you can close your eyes for a few seconds down the long side and feel the balance that comes out of that corner when the movement is executed correctly. In this particular situation, you might notice your animal starting to fall in slightly to the inside after you close your eyes. A squeeze-release from the inside leg, sending your mule forward and into the outside rein, corrects the balance and keeps him straight down the long side.

Your seat bones are closest to your body's center of gravity, making them the best sensors of balance. "Feel" the weight shift from one seat bone to the other through turns and circles, then even out as you ride straight lines and diagonals. You soon discover that in order to do a circle in better balance, you must have slightly more weight on the outside seat bone. This situates your weight over the outside hind leg, which is the impulsing leg. Putting the weight over the outside hind leg clears the shoulders for freer movement in front. If you ride on your *inside* seat bone, the weight begins to fall to the inside of the circle, inhibiting the upright, forward balance.

I repeat—plan your course of action! You cannot expect your mule to maintain his balance when he is constantly being surprised with changes of direction or gait. Use your eyes correctly to enhance your balance and to help you plan your course more realistically. Teach yourself to be accurate with your eyes. Look well ahead at all times, and try to stay exactly on the lines and the arcs of your circles. When you plan a circle, look halfway around your circle at a time so that you can make both halves equal with minimal trouble. Keep your eyes on a visual horizontal line that runs parallel to the ground. Remember—you have two eyes, and any movement as slight as a tip of the head to one side or the other can affect the upright balance of your mule. Dropping your eyes to the ground shifts your mule's balance forward and onto the shoulders, again interrupting his balance.

Do small circles, but only as small as your mule can handle without losing his balance. When he maintains his balance easily and without interruption, you can begin to decrease the size of the circles. Keep movements planned and large. This will give your mule plenty of response time through planned movements and will allow you to ride and correct the balance more easily yourself. If for some reason your mule bumbles, falls out, or rushes, stop him with even pressure on both reins. Back him up slowly and deliberately, one step at a time, then calmly go back and try to repeat the movement. If he makes the same mistake a second time, halt, back up, then walk through the area that is giving you the problem. Resume trotting or cantering when you are through. When you approach that area again, slow him down again, go through, and resume your plan.

If he "ducks out" with you and begins to run, keep your connection on the rein that he has pulled as best as you can, and try to stop him by pulling on both reins together. Verbally, try to calm him, and when he finally stops, praise him for stopping. Then, turn him with the rein that he has just pulled out of your hand, and return him to the task. Do *not* try to pull him around with the other rein, because this will cause him to lose his balance and will frighten him even more. If he is praised for stopping, he will not be afraid to stop. If he's punished for running, he may never *want* to stop.

The main goal is to cultivate a mule that is between and responsive to your aids—to your seat, to your legs, and to your hands. If you keep your eyes focused ahead and your hands and legs evenly balanced over your seat bones, you can strongly affect your mule's vertical balance. Your use of the aids correctly and repetitively will eventually allow your mule to become lighter in the bridle and more responsive. In addition, his muscles will begin to condition properly. An animal that is restrained and forced will develop muscles incorrectly. In turn, this will cause him stiffness through many movements. Most commonly, you see a slight "U" in the base of the neck in front of the withers. This is caused by stiffness in the poll from riding from front to back rather than from back to front. Actually, the stiffness will transmit to other parts of the body, but the most obvious signs show in the neck and poll. Incorrect development of the muscles will undoubtedly inhibit your mule's best performance.

I ride my equines diagonally through the aids to get the best lateral and vertical response. I want to maintain a good forward movement, which means that the impulsion must come from the hindquarters and from the push forward. Think of your hands and legs as four corners of the same box that contains your mule. If you push forward on one side at a time from, say, left leg to left hand, it leaves the other whole side of the animal unchecked, and he will proceed forward with a tendency to drift into the "open" side. This is why you ride from back to front, leg to hand, in a diagonal fashion— it pushes your mule from the outside leg forward into a straight and balanced inside rein, and from the inside leg to the outside rein. He remains upright on the arcs and sufficiently bent. The wider the space between your legs and between your hands, the more lateral "play" you will feel in your mule. If you keep your hands close together and your legs snugly around his barrel, there is a lot less lateral "play" and a great deal more accuracy on your patterns.

But what if he will not turn without your really pulling on the inside rein? He will turn if you do it correctly. Remember—it doesn't matter how far you turn his head to the side. It isn't attached to the ground, and he will only go where his legs go! You will be fairly safe if you always try to keep his head and neck

Meredith Hodges and Lucky Three Mae Bea C.T. in the victory gallop at the Abbe Ranch Horse Trials.

straight, in front of his shoulders. When you wish to turn, give a slight half-halt to slow for the turn. Be sure to support your mule with your legs as you do this; the inside leg should become stronger with each squeeze and give with each release. Keep your outside rein checked back slightly compared to your inside rein, which pulls and releases, and hold your hand in close to the withers on the outside. Do not check too hard or your mule will turn out instead of around the circle. Take your inside rein away from the withers a little to encourage the turn, but be careful not to take it any farther than necessary, because this will disconnect your mule's hindquarters from his shoulders. As you do this repeatedly, your mule will learn to bend his body to the arc of the circle and not just his head and neck.

The finer you tune your own aids, the lighter and more responsive your mule will become. To summarize: Plan your course of action; in the beginning, keep movements large and flowing; keep your eyes looking ahead; and keep your aids even and close in laterally while being strong and encouraging from back to front vertically. Do not be too concerned about where your mule's nose is if his body is correct. As he becomes more confident, fit, and relaxed, and as your aids become more correct, the head and neck will drop on their own accord. If you set the head and neck before the body has been conditioned to balance and round, you will produce an animal with a hollow back and a lot of vertical and lateral stiffness. This will not even allow him to respond to your aids correctly if he wants to, because he is physically unable to do so. It may take a little longer to condition your body and his body correctly, but the result is a sound, cooperative animal, possessing the mental and physical qualities necessary for the best performance upon your request.

Meredith Hodges and Ruth Elkins, from Great Britain, on a trail ride.

CHAPTER XXIX

Attitudes and Use of Restraints

There has been much discussion about training mules versus training horses. Some say that mules are harder to train than horses, while others say just the opposite. In my experience, it isn't really that one is more difficult than the other, because they both have their individual limitations. For instance, if a horse does not wish to comply in a given situation, he can be more easily bullied into complying than a mule or donkey. On the other hand, when you teach a mule or donkey an exercise on one day, he usually remembers what he has been taught and complies more easily regardless of how many days or weeks pass between lessons. The horse, on the other hand, tends to forget. What all this amounts to is that one is really not more easily trained than the other. What really makes the difference is the experience, the knowledge, and the attitude of the trainer.

Mules and donkeys, sensitive and intelligent creatures that they are, seem to be more concerned than horses about the overall attitude of the trainer. They do not take kindly to punitive action. This negative reinforcement more often brings about fear and resistance rather than a positive response. In order to modify the mule's behavior in a positive way, you must keep punishment to the barest minimum and emphasize positive reinforcement. It is much easier to modify the behavior of any equine by being intelligent, maintaining a positive attitude, and using restraints correctly.

When a mule does not comply with your wishes, your first reaction may be to get angry or frustrated. If you think about it, getting angry is really no solution to the problem. If this were a person with whom you were having a misunderstanding, what would you do to persuade that individual that you were correct? First, you need to get his attention; therefore, you might say or do something to temper his defensive attitude. emphasizing your concern for him politely and considerately. Finally, you might allow him time to respond.

This is no different from what you need to do with your mule. Being intelligent about a situation minimizes negative reactive responses; politeness and consideration promote an overall positive attitude on both parts and open the lines of communication.

This animal outweighs you by several hundred pounds, which means that you must sometimes use restraints carefully and correctly to perpetuate the close relationship between you and your mule in the training environment. Use restraints to help "explain" what you wish to your mule, but do not use them as a perpetual crutch. Always be intelligent, maintain a positive attitude, and use restraints carefully to promote successful training sessions.

Many restraints are available for use in the equine industry today: martingales, tie-downs, side reins, draw reins, hobbles, and many others. In my estimation, these restraints are being used much too freely as crutches and are responsible for terrible body posture and limited responsiveness among equines today. A restraint should be used as a tool to help you attain a positive response from your animal. Once you get the proper response, it is your responsibility to phase out the restraint in order to instill the correct behavior itself in your animal. In the case of the mule, it doesn't take five minutes for him to figure out when the restraint is not present. Therefore, if his response depends on the restraint itself, you have literally wasted your time.

The most universally abused restraint today probably is the draw rein. People seem to be in such a hurry to get an equine's head down that they seem to forget about the animal's overall body posture. Consequently, you will see many equines traveling with their head down, yet they look stiff and stilted through the gaits. If you have done your homework and cultivated a strong, forward movement in your mule, initiated from the hindquarters, the use of draw reins for a day or so can be helpful. Assess the problem with the animal, then decide the proper adjustment for the draw reins. If the mule carries his head unusually high, you might need to fasten the draw reins as low as between the legs. If he isn't particularly high-headed but tends to stick his nose out when you squeeze with your legs, you may need to just fasten the draw reins at the girth on either side to keep his head in a more correct position.

These adjustments can change often from situation to situation and from animal to animal;

Everybody always has to know what's going on!

for this reason, it is essential to evaluate your goals before proceeding with restraints. Use your draw reins to give you leverage that will hold your mule's head steady, and use your legs (and crop, if necessary) to drive him forward into the bridle. When he complies, soften your hands. Do not pull the animal's head down and pull him back over his haunches—this *cannot* facilitate good posture! With the use of the draw reins, you will receive the response that you wish to create. Your mule now has an idea about what you expect from him, and he can begin to take responsibility for the action himself.

In early training, when a young mule is taught to "go" as you squeeze with your legs, he sticks his nose out and goes. Good posture, however, needs to be cultivated. By using the draw reins correctly (i.e., squeezing your reins and legs simultaneously as the outside hind leg comes forward, then releasing with the forward movement from the inside hind leg), you indicate to your mule that he can still go forward from your legs, but that he must flex and arc his back to carry your weight in the most energy efficient manner. You will enhance his way of going so that he will be more comfortable.

Now that you have shown him a better way to move, give him time to figure it out for himself and to take responsibility for his own body carriage. At first, his muscles may not be as elastic as you would like, and he may not be able to carry himself correctly for long periods of time. If you are patient and understanding of his dilemma (he wants to please but is not physically able to comply 100 percent), and you keep giving him the same cues without the restraint, he soon will be able to oblige you. Too often, results are expected from mules too quickly. Improper use of mechanical restraints can cause body soreness and negative responses in equines. Be aware of this, and keep your expectations realistic.

If you realize that correct development of mind and muscle takes time, you can relax and let the mule learn at his own pace. You can utilize these helpful restraints to minimize resistance in difficult situations and actually enjoy the training process. Use restraints only to show him what to do, then go back to the reins as soon as possible.

The most helpful restraint with mules and donkeys is the scotch hobble (see illustration). This restraint helps to facilitate good ground manners in the animal by restraining a hind foot. This causes the mule to stand still while you work on him, whether it's clipping, shoeing, or saddling him for the first time. As with any restraint, it must be phased out sooner or later.

How, you ask, do you phase out a restraint? You probably will have to use a restraint in its full capacity the first time to get the desired response. You should use draw reins in conjunction with your regular reins and make connection with the draw reins only when necessary; in the beginning, that might mean every stride. It is obvious how you can withdraw from use of the draw reins, but what about a restraint like the scotch hobble, which is a seemingly inflexible arrangement?

A scotch hobble is a nonslip knot tied around the neck. Leaving about eight feet of rope, you go down around a hind foot and back to the neck loop, then down around the hind foot again. You then go back to the neck loop and tie off with a quick release knot. When you catch the hind foot, make sure that it is pulled forward enough so that his toe just starts to leave the ground. This prevents him from tiring too quickly on three legs, yet inhibits his kicking ability. This procedure is also helpful when handling the hind feet, because you can grab the rope and pull the foot to you, keeping your head and upper body away from the danger zone.

The first time that you use the scotch hobble, you probably will have to secure the hind foot so that it cannot touch the ground. As your mule becomes more quiet and accepting of what you are doing, you can loosen the scotch hobble a little each session. If he is good, adjust it so that his toe rests on the ground. Next time, you may be able to let him rest on all fours, with the rope tied loosely into position. You can do this until he complies to the point where the rope is actually around only the hind foot and is lying loosely on the ground. Naturally, if he becomes fidgety, back up one step and tighten your connections on the rope. When your mule stands quietly without the scotch hobble, you have phased out the restraint.

Choosing the right restraint for a given situation takes thought and consideration. You must ask yourself, what restraints are available? Which restraint will most likely bring about the response that I desire from my mule? Will the response with this restraint come with little or no resistance, and is it humane? Will it cause other problems in the animal that might be difficult to deal with? And finally, can it be phased out relatively easily? Keeping these points in mind when using restraints will help to prevent your relationship with your mule from becoming a battleground. Bear in mind that the restraint required may vary from situation to situation and from animal to animal; therefore, consider your options carefully. Remember—using intelligence, maintaining a good attitude, and using restraints correctly can greatly enhance the training experience!

A set of hobbles, a scotch rope, and draw reins are just about all that you need to restrain your mule without tranquilizing him.

Hobbles should be nonabrasive to the pasterns.

The elbow-pull is useful for those who have problems with draw reins.

To employ the scotch hobble, tie a nonslip knot around the neck of your mule using the end of a long (fifteen-foot) rope. Take the excess down to the hind foot and around the pastern, then back up through the loop around the neck and back around the pastern a second time. Wrap the excess around the ropes going to the foot and back up to the loop around the neck again, and tie with a quick-release knot. By wrapping the ropes going to the foot, you prevent your mule from freeing his foot from the ropes. This restraint can be used in almost any situation where you require your mule to stand still.

To use the face tie, wrap your lead around once until his face is over and tight against the rail.

Then, slip the rope through the noseband of the halter and around the hitchrail again and secure it.

This technique is useful in working around very young mules, although it works on adults as well. You must remember to just step back if he begins to struggle; give him space to learn the situation.

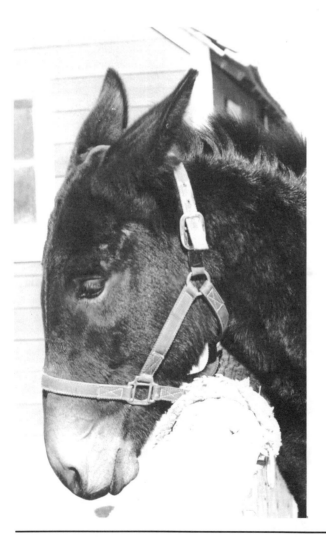

Although the saddles seem very different, various adjustments for the draw rein can be found . . .

for the mule that carries his head too low,

or, for the mule that carries his head too high.

The elbow-pull has pressure points at the poll, the mouth, the underarms, and over the withers. If he rounds correctly, he will feel nothing.

Draw reins can be attached high on the saddle for a mule that tends to carry his head too low.

Or, they can be adjusted a little lower for the mule that tends to carry his head too high.

Meredith Hodges and Lucky Three Mae Bea C.T. at Bishop Mule Days, 1990; third-place World Champion 1st Level Dressage Mule (Lucky Three Ciji took Reserve Champion).

CHAPTER XXX

Grooming and Clipping for Show

People have often asked me how on earth can only three people—my daughter, my husband, and myself—manage to prepare and show as many as eighteen mules and donkeys for one show. They say that we must be crazy (and maybe we are a little crazy!), but a few simple rules of organization make this possible.

The first consideration is grooming the animals. Anyone who body clips an animal knows how tedious and time-consuming this is. Mule and donkey hair does not appear to grow back as quickly, nor as radically, as horse hair. Therefore, you can clip your mule or donkey two to three weeks in advance of your show and do touch-up work just before the show. If you have no shows until summer, you may want to body clip in mid-April anyway. It is at this time that the winter hair begins to shed and the summer hair starts to come in. If you clip off the winter hair and blanket your animal for the remainder of the spring, the hair that grows in will be much more manageable than the heavy winter hair, and this will greatly reduce grooming time before the show. Once the heavier coat is eliminated, a weekly grooming keeps his coat nicely maintained; daily, or every other day, is even better.

Each time that you groom him before riding, check and clip as needed the muzzle hairs, the hair around the eyes and the ears, and the hair around the coronet bands. Leave the hair inside the ears to prevent irritation from bugs and flies, but trim the outside edges and backs of the ears.

An ounce of corn oil in his feed daily will assure a sheen in his coat on show day without the use of artificial highlighters. Trimming, or shoeing, your mule on a regular six-to-eight-week schedule will assure that his feet will not need attending at the last minute. A routine vaccination, worming, Coggins testing, and permanent brand inspection will ready him for transport to any show anywhere. All that remains to be done right before the show is minor clipping, bathing, and hoof polishing.

Each individual mule or donkey should have his own personal show halter and bridle for convenience. Driving animals should each have their own set of harness. This reduces the time between tack changes while at the show.

189

Dress rehearsals before the show at home are beneficial. Prepare as if you are about to enter each class, one at a time. First, pick the clothing that you need to wear, and store it in a designated place in your house. Do not actually wear it for the rehearsal. As you choose the items, take note of what needs to be cleaned or polished, and set them aside. Then, tack up your animal, checking each piece of equipment to make sure that it is in working order.

Go ahead and practice the class. As you untack your mule, set the tack aside from the rest in your tack room for cleaning later. Do this for each animal in each class.

Your animals will be better at the show if they get plenty of rest before the show. It is wise to spend the day before the show cleaning your tack, clothes, and equipment. Before you begin to clean, load all of the items into your trailer that are ready to go without cleaning. Then, as you clean the remaining items, load them directly into the trailer as you finish them.

When the basic gear for you and your animal is loaded, make a checklist for feed, buckets, hoses, brushes, forks, brooms, shovels, and other equipment that you will need for general care. Load them and check them off. When you have finished, lay out all the items that you will need for transport (i.e., sheets, blankets, shipping boots, etc.) so that they are easily available. If you proceed in this manner, you minimize the risk of forgetting any important items.

It is best to make sure that your trailer is fully loaded (except for the animals) the night before you leave, because this gives you overnight to think of any item that you might have missed. Gear such as your ice chest can be left until morning, or until the last minute, provided that you put it in a highly visible spot with a list of what is to be put in it. Do not try to rely on your memory, because it will be clouded by the excitement and anticipation of the show.

If you are taking a number of mules and donkeys to the show, it is wise to bathe them with soap at home the day before. Then, cover the animal with a sheet or blanket and leg wraps. The day of the show, you then only need to rinse

Meredith Hodges and Lucky Three Ciji, Colorado Classic Open and Mule Sidesaddle Champion.

or vacuum any excess dirt. This minimizes grooming time at the show.

Post the show schedule where you will be tacking up for each class, and organize your clothing and equipment so that it is ready to go and is easily accessible. Once the show actually begins, you will not have time to go hunting for misplaced items.

Take note of your clothing changes, and wear clothes that are easily changed. For instance, if your Western classes are before your English classes, you can wear your breeches underneath your Western slacks and chaps. You can easily change from English attire to driving and side-saddle attire by wearing your English clothing, then changing your headgear and adding a lap rug for driving or apron for side-

Eagle Rest Don Quixote, from Brayer Hill Farm, Boyd, Texas, shown by Sue King.

Brayer Hill Bubba, from Brayer Hill Farm, Boyd, Texas, ridden by Dennis Lee.

saddle. Changing your boots is pretty much optional, because English boots are easily hidden beneath properly fitting Western chaps and are appropriate footwear for English, driving, and side-saddle.

If classes are spaced together fairly closely and you are using more than one animal, it is wise to tack up the other animals ahead of time so that they are ready to go. If you are using only one saddle for more than one animal, the other animals can still be bridled with the halter slipped over it. This way, they can be tied and waiting. Be sure to tie up the reins so that they will not be chewed or stepped on. If you are using the same mule throughout the show, tacking and stripping should not be too time-consuming if your equipment is well organized.

Showing should be fun and exciting, but it can easily turn into a nightmare when things are out of place and chaotic. Make your motel and stabling reservations early, and leave for the show well ahead of schedule to allow for breakdowns or other unforeseen emergencies. By all means, bring friends to help you, but give them a briefing and a list of jobs that they can do. They won't be much help if they have to keep asking what to do the day of the show. If you

are going any distance at all, have your truck and trailer checked thoroughly before you leave. There is nothing more frustrating than a major breakdown on the roadside with a trailer full of animals!

To summarize, with routine grooming, farrier care, veterinarian care, and permanent brand inspections, you can greatly reduce your show preparation time. Dress rehearsals, individual tack for each animal, and organized loading will assure that all of your tack and equipment will be readily available. Advanced motel and stabling reservations will afford you and your animals much needed rest when you arrive. Having your truck and trailer checked before you leave will make sure that you arrive in plenty of time. And, organization of tack and equipment when you do arrive will heighten the chances for an enjoyable and relaxing show.

How should you groom a mule for show? When you bring the mule into the barn for grooming, tie him up and take a few steps back to make an overall assessment of what must be done. The main consideration is the amount and kind of clipping required. Body clippings in the late fall or winter months are unadvisable unless you have the proper facilities to keep the mule warm and dry. But let's say it is the beginning of summer. Your next consideration, after deciding to clip, is the length of the natural coat and the condition of the hair. If the hair is long but the coat dry and coarse, you probably want to body clip the mule going *with* the hair to get rid of the dry ends only. If the mule has long, shiny hair, you may want to go *against* the hair to expose the shiny undercoat when you are finished. The mule with relatively short hair does not need to be body clipped; you only need to touch up the areas that need it. When deciding whether or not to body clip, consider how difficult it will be to blend the natural hair with the clipped areas. (For example, after clipping the legs, can you tie in the shoulders and the hips smoothly so that the coat is one continuous surface?) When you have decided what needs to be done, you are ready to begin.

Before clipping, it is wise to clean the animal so that dirt and dust do not get into your clippers and clog them. Give the animal a quick bath and let him dry thoroughly, or give him a going over with a curry comb, a dandy brush, and a vacuum to remove loosened dust and dirt. Now you are ready to begin clipping.

It is wise to begin with the head and legs. These are the most difficult areas to do, and you do not want to have to struggle with these areas after the mule has had a chance to become tired and irritable. Save the easiest for last. When doing the head, pay special attention to long facial hairs, such as the eyebrows, the muzzle, and the hairs under the jaws—they should be clean-shaven. If the animal pulls away when you are doing the ears, use a humane twitch to hold his head in place. Generally, this is all you need. Never ear-down a mule! Unlike horses, mules will not forget over time who was responsible for the pain, especially when it involves the ears.

When you are finished with the head, direct your attention to the mane. Ask yourself if this mule has a manageable mane or not. If he has a fairly nice mane, you may want to leave it and the foretop and just clip the bridle path. If you do leave the mane, make sure that it is pulled to Quarterhorse length or even a bit shorter, but not any longer. Allow a decent length

for braiding. Pull the foretop so that it is relatively short and thin and does *not* resemble a bush between the ears. Instead, you want to have a feathery appearance. The standard Western procedure these days, however, is simply to roach the foretop and bridle path, then cut the rest of the mane as straight as you can at about one-half inch. Leave it longer for braiding with the English procedure.

The tail is another area with a few variations. There are three basic ways to do the mule's tail, all of which are acceptable in the show ring. The first and most prevalent way is to simply shave the short tail hairs at the base of the tail down about two inches. Use this procedure only if the mule has short hair or if he is totally body clipped, because it is difficult to blend long hair from the croup into the bald tail base.

The second method is to bell the tail in three tiers. This method is strictly a matter of preference, and unless the mule has a fairly thick tail, do not attempt to bell it.

The third way to groom the tail is my personal preference. Apply baby oil to the base of the tail on a daily basis, and comb through it with some kind of tail brush. (I use a human wig brush because it doesn't break the hairs.) This gives the tail a smooth and natural appearance and keeps it sufficiently conditioned. It also gives your animal longer hairs at the tail base to braid for English performances.

Next, do the legs. Chestnuts and ergots can be removed to a manageable size by soaking them in baby oil and then peeling them off at skin level. You may have to use a knife to peel them off, but be sure to moisturize them or they may bleed. I usually clip *against* the hair on the legs because it gives a neater, trimmer appearance. Clip a clean line around the coronet band, and be careful clipping the hair between the bones in the leg. If blending is to be done, clip against the hair on the leg to just above the knee, and use the hair on the forearm and gaskin to blend down to the leg. If the mule is to be completely body clipped against the hair, no blending will be necessary.

As the final step in clipping, do the rest of the body as you have decided, either with

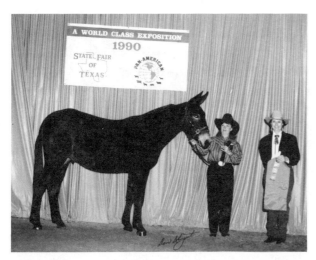

Brayer Hill Sure Smooth Zorro, from Brayer Hill Farm, Boyd, Texas, shown by Sue King.

the hair or against it. When blending, go with the hair. Pay close attention to the fuzzy areas under the belly, around the forearms, and around the buttocks.

After clipping, bathe the mule all over with a recommended horse shampoo. Be sure to bathe all those hard-to-reach places, such as the nostrils and genitals, gently so as not to irritate the mule. The bath will remove excess dirt, dust, and oil residue from the clippers. Remove all of the soap because dried soap dulls the coat. Now he is ready for the final stages of show grooming.

If the mule needs a little more shine to his coat, you may want to use a conditioning product, which should be applied while the mule is still damp. If you are going to be riding him, do not use these products over his back, because they will cause your saddle to slip. In this instance, apply it to the head, the mane, the tail, and the legs only. As mentioned earlier, artificial highlighters are unnecessary if you use one ounce of corn oil in his feed daily. This will produce a natural sheen and will aid in digestion.

When the mule is dry, go over him with a curry comb and dandy brush to remove the last of the dust and dirt. Check for hairs that might have been missed during clipping and clip them.

Then clean the mule's feet thoroughly. Hoof black is still widely used on the feet after they have been cleaned, but I prefer to enhance the feet by using a natural protein on them such as bacon grease. The bacon grease gives them the desired shiny and oily appearance without drying out the feet. If dust adheres to the hoof, it can easily be wiped clean with a rag before you enter the arena. If you use Hoof black, be sure to use a hoof moisturizer to keep the hooves from drying out while the product wears off.

Finally, use a generous amount of baby oil on the face, the head, and the ears, especially highlighting the eyes and the muzzle. If the mule has black socks, highlight them too with the baby oil. If highlighting white socks, it is best to stick with a less oily product, as the dust will come off more readily. Apply a small amount of baby oil to the base of the tail and comb it through. Then use the same brush over the mane and foretop for mild conditioning and shine. Now rub him all over with a dry towel to put the finishing shine on him and to absorb any excess oil left on the coat. And now, you are ready for the show ring.

Bishop Mule Days Donkey Pleasure Class.

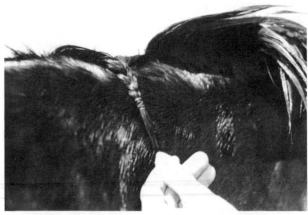

If your mule has a decent mane, you may want to consider braiding it for show. This is especially useful if your mule's mane does not fall on only one side. Braids can be done for both Western and English. Section your braids about one and one-fourth inches apart, as shown in the photo. Allow Western braids to hang with a tassel of loose hair on the ends, as shown in the photos.

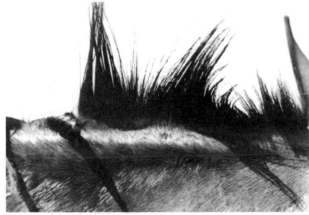

Be sure to keep the mane damp with water or with some kind of setting gel to catch the whispy ends in the section that you are braiding.

Although his mane may have long and short spots, use a setting gel to help you gather all of these hairs together in a tight, clean braid.

When you section off the hair for your braid, use your comb to make sure that the line across the crest of his neck is straight, because it will show.

Then, split the hairs in three equal sections to start your braiding.

As you braid each section of hair, be sure to pull downward to cause the braids to lie flat against your mule's neck.

Use your comb to hold back the unbraided part of the mane to avoid a lot of whispy stray ends.

Be sure to pull downward as you put the band on the braid, or you may find your hairs loosening and the braid standing up rather than lying flat.

If you have braided the mane tightly and downward, the other side will look like this.

Using a bucket or small footstool will help you to get tall enough to make braiding easier.

For Western events, leave the braids in long strands, as shown in the photo. If you want to have a less sparse effect, make your braid sections smaller than one and one-fourth inches.

To complete your braids for English competition, take each small braid, double it in half, and turn the tail of the braid under. Then conceal it in the base of the braid.

Once it is in position, secure it with a rubber band.

Do each braid in this manner.

If you have problems getting your braids to stand up on the neck a little, so that they show on both sides, leave the tail of the braid against the neck, as shown in the photo.

Once your mane braiding is finished, you may want to slick some setting gel on the entire job to catch any whispy ends that you may have missed.

The braided foretop is done in the same way and can be left to hang. Or it can be balled up and banded.

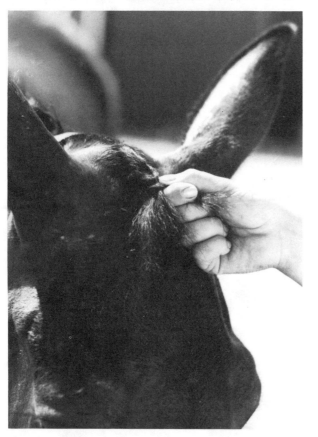

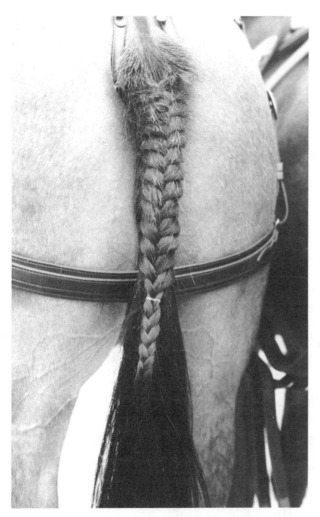

The base tail hairs on a mule can be very difficult to catch in a French braid, but if you braid with very small sections, you can catch most of it. The rest can be encouraged to lie flat with setting gel.

The tail of the braid on the tail is generally looped under and banded to give a neater appearance.

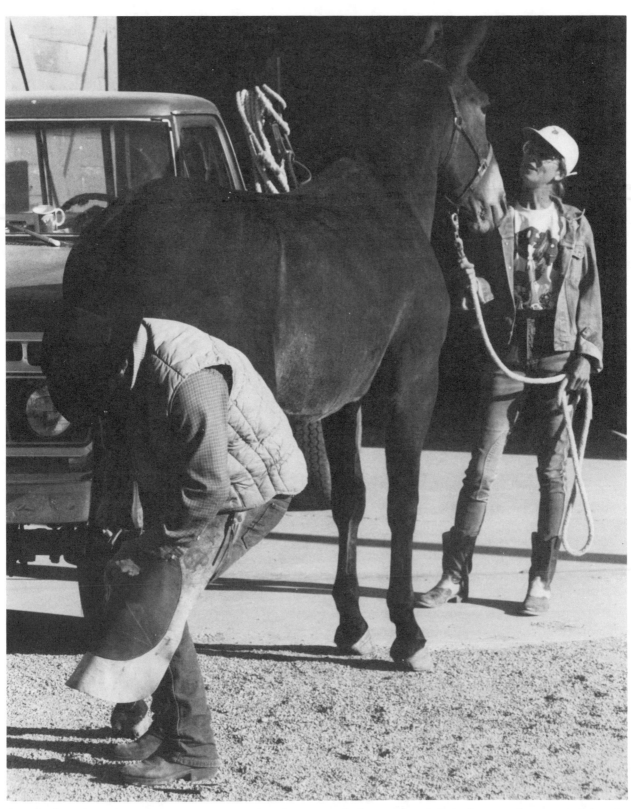

Jerry Banks making shoes for the Lucky Three mules. Having a mule that stands quietly is always a pleasure. A sheltered, clean work area is also preferred.

CHAPTER XXXI

Responsibilities to the Veterinarian and Farrier

Mule owners today carry a tremendous amount of responsibility. Not only are they obligated to promote their animals through breeding and performance in order to educate people on the mule's outstanding abilities, but they also must exhibit the animal's manageability on a day-to-day basis with veterinarians and horseshoers.

Many veterinarians and horseshoers refuse to work on mules. Some are slaves to the old wives' tales about mules being stubborn, ornery, and dangerous, and some are subject to owners who cannot manage their own animals. These professionals studied primarily with horses and are more apt to be tolerant of a misbehaving horse than of a misbehaving mule simply because they have a better idea of what to expect and how to deal with it. These professionals deal with us regularly and carry stories and opinions throughout the equine world, and it is of primary importance that their thoughts and ideas about mules be positive, at least for the most part. It is your responsibility as a mule owner to educate these professionals by making their interaction with your mule a pleasant experience.

Veterinarians and horseshoers agree on many of their complaints about equine owners: (1) often the animal is not up and ready for treatment upon their arrival; (2) the animals are not handled regularly and therefore are difficult to treat; (3) owners use excitable disciplinary tactics while the professional is working on the animal, putting him in physical jeopardy; and (4) owners do not follow up on treatment instructions. True, these complaints apply to both horse and mule owners, but if mule owners are to dispel old rumors about mules, it is twice as important that they have a manageable animal. The veterinarian or horseshoer will not be as quick to forgive a mule.

Your mule must therefore learn to lead easily, to stand quietly, and to accept touch all over his body, especially about the head, the ears, and other sensitive areas. To accomplish this, only a few things need to be done. First, you must gain the confidence and trust of your mule—be his friend. When this bond is formed, you can proceed

201

with confidence. Teach him to lead as you would teach any young equine, but reward him when he does well. This does not cause bad habits in mules if done purposefully. Once he leads easily, try to bring him in a few times a week and spend time grooming him and caring for his feet. This accustoms him to being handled.

If he is the nervous type, he probably requires desensitization. Tie him up with a stout halter and lead. (I often use a lunge line tied around the neck with a nonslip knot, then a loop over the nose and a tie to a stout post. Do not use the snaps!) Use a small tarp or plastic, or a material of this caliber, that is spooky and a little noisy. Begin by showing it to him, let him sniff it to identify it as a harmless object, and then slowly shake it a little and rub him all over with it from head to tail and on both sides. When he is comfortable with the

Dena Hodges and Rambling Rose, National Western Stock Show, 1989, Sidesaddle Champion.

rubbing, you can begin slapping him with it over his body, then pulling it over his head and down his nose. Increase the impact of the slapping until he stands quietly for it with a minimum amount of twitching. Do not expect to accomplish this in one day. This procedure should be done in stages every time you handle your mule until he has accepted it and other types of handling with no trouble.

If your mule does not settle when he is tied, you may have to hobble his front feet to partially immobilize him. Make sure that the ground is not too hard, because he may go down in the hobbles. But do not be afraid to put the hobbles on. Mules are smart, and it doesn't take them but a few minutes to discover the purpose of the hobbles. If your mule is a kicker, you may have to scotch-hobble him. (See the instructions for scotch hobbling on page 152.)

To accustom your mule to being handled about the head, simply make it a point to keep his bridle path trimmed with either clippers or scissors. Usually, only one restraint is needed for difficult animals; in this case, it would be a humane twitch. If you are fairly coordinated, you can hold the twitch with one hand while you clip with the other. If you are not, recruit an assistant. It is always safer to have someone on hand anyway. Do not use chain twitches on mules. Mules have a low tolerance to pain and will fight back when the pain becomes too severe.

The most effective form of restraint probably is the horse chute. A word of caution: The mule should be used to having his feet handled outside the chute before you try it while he is in the chute. Also, be sure that his head is secured so that he cannot jump out. Remember—mules can jump from a standstill! The chute offers the ultimate in safety for you, for the vet, and in some cases, for even the horseshoer.

If your mule is accustomed to this type of handling, you should experience little difficulty in getting him treated. But if he does become difficult, do your professional a courtesy and ask him to stand aside before you discipline your mule. Proceed when the animal is again calm.

In following up treatment, make sure that you follow instructions. Sometimes, treatment can be difficult, but rest assured that the mule will better tolerate treatment each time if he is dealt with firmly and fairly. Thus, your job will get easier each time.

Above all, make sure that a handler is available to your vet or shoer when he comes so that he can do the best job possible for you and your mule. He is not a trainer or handler—that is your responsibility! If these guidelines are observed, your professional's job will be much easier. Your animal will get the treatment that he needs, and the stories from farm to farm about mule clients will improve.

Clients are not the only ones at fault. They also have their complaints about professionals: (1) they're not on time; (2) they don't explain the problem; (3) they're too rough on the animals; and (4) they do not facilitate client participation in treatment. The key is that this is the age of specialization. As a veterinarian or horseshoer, you are fully aware of your professional capabilities, but are you aware that owners also have their areas of expertise? Their animal is usually one of those areas! As a professional courtesy, clients should be called when appointment times need to be changed. And as a gesture of consideration, clients should be informed regarding the diagnosis and treatment of their animals. Communicating with your client in this manner helps him to help you. If clients are informed, they can deal with lesser problems themselves, leaving the professionals to tend to more severe and important cases. Also, if the client is informed, he is more apt to be meticulous in follow-up treatment. Good communication facilitates successful treatment and leaves less room for error.

Respect the professionalism of your client. He is with your patient most of the time and is aware of psychological aspects that might come into play. Ask your client how an animal might best be handled for a given treatment. If he isn't sure, by all means proceed as you know best. But if he does know, respect him as the handler/trainer, just as he respects you as the veterinarian or horseshoer. Only by mutual respect and communication can the common purpose of caring for the patients be fulfilled. And mule owners—try twice as hard to fulfill your responsibilities; lots of ignorant tales need to be put to rest!

Meredith and Dena Hodges with Mae Bea C.T. and Ciji — goodbye. Friendship and respect will cultivate the best in anyone, even a mule.

Left and right: Borium shoes by Jerry Banks, Loveland, Colorado, farrier.

The donkeys at the Lucky Three prefer to be done as a family. A bucket of grain keeps them occupied and minimizes fussing and kicking. It's better to give in to a few simple needs of your longears, particularly with donkeys, than it is to start a fight that you can't possibly win.

Even something as obnoxious as floating his teeth can be done easily if you are patient and use a certain amount of common sense.

A confining chute can be useful for all kinds of vetting and breeding.

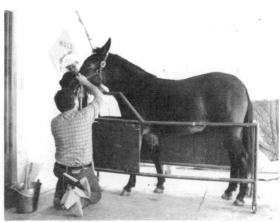

Mytikas thanks K. M. Knebel, DVM, for giving her back a happy and healthy Lucky Three Melinda's Masterpiece.

A good vet for your mule will respect your knowledge of your animal and will give you the benefit of his knowledge. Your mule's vet is like your own family doctor. Spend time looking for a vet who will earn your trust and that of your mule.

Which one's for me?

Glossary

Breeching: The part of the harness that goes around the haunches.

Cadence: The beat, time or measure of rhythmical motion or activity.

Canter:
1. The canter is a pace of "three time," where at canter to the right, for instance, the footfalls follow one another as follows: left hind, left diagonal (simultaneously left fore and right hind), right fore, followed by a movement of suspension with all four feet in the air before the next stride begins.
2. The canter always with light, cadenced and regular strides, should be moved into without hesitation.
3. The quality of the canter is judged by the general impression, the regularity and lightness of the three time pace—originating in the acceptance of the bridle with a supple poll and in the engagement of the hindquarters with an active hock action—and by the ability of maintaining the same rhythm and a natural balance even after a transition from one canter to another. The horse should always remain straight on straight lines.
4. The following canters are recognized: working canter, collected canter, medium canter and extended canter.
   (Article 1905, AHSA Rulebook 1992-93)

Collected canter: The horse remaining on the bit moves forward with his neck raised and arched. The collected canter is marked by the lightness of the forehand and the engagement of the hindquarters, i.e., is characterized by supple, free and mobile shoulders and very active quarters. The horse's strides are shorter than at the other canters but he is lighter and more mobile.

Extended canter: The horse covers as much ground as possible. Maintaining the same rhythm he lengthens his strides to the utmost without losing any of his calmness and lightness as a result of great impulsion from the hind-quarters. The rider allows the horse remaining on the bit without leaning on it to lower and extend his head and neck; the tip of his nose pointing more or less forward.

Medium canter: This is a pace between the working and the extended canter. The horse goes forward with free, balanced and moderately extended strides and an obvious impulsion from the hind-quarters. The rider allows the horse remaining on the bit to carry his head a little more in front of the vertical than at the collected and working canter and allows him at the same time to lower his head and neck slightly. The strides should be long and as even as possible and the whole movement balanced and unconstrained.

Working canter: This is a pace between the collected and the medium canter in which a horse, not yet trained and ready for collected movements, shows himself properly balanced and remaining on the bit, goes forward with even, light and cadenced strides and good hock action. The expression "good hock action" does not mean that collection is a required quality of the working canter. It only underlines the importance of an impulsion originated from the activity of the hindquarters. The cadence in the transitions from medium canter as well as from extended canter to collected canter should be maintained.

Change of Leg Through the Trot: This is a change of leg where the horse is brought back into the trot and after two, or at the most three steps, is restarted into a canter with the other leg leading.

Counter-Canter ("False Canter"): This is a movement where the rider, for instance on a circle to the left, deliberately makes his horse canter with the right canter lead (with the right fore leading). The counter-canter is a suppling movement. The horse maintains his natural flexion at the poll to the outside of the circle, in other words, is bent to the side of the leading leg. His conformation does not permit his spine to be bent to the line of the circle. The rider avoiding any contortion causing contraction and disorder should especially endeavor to limit the deviation of the quarters to the outside of the circle and restrict his demands according to the degree of suppleness of the horse.

Flying Change of Leg or Change of Leg in the Air: This change of leg is executed in close connection with the suspension which follows each stride of the canter. Flying changes of leg can also be executed in series, for instance at every 4th, 3rd, 2nd or at every stride. The horse even in the series remains light, calm and straight with lively impulsion, maintaining the same rhythm and balance throughout the series concerned. In order not to restrict or restrain the lightness and fluency of the flying changes of leg in series, the degree of collection should be slightly less than otherwise at collected canter.

Simple Change of Leg at Canter: This is a change of leg where the horse is brought back into the walk and, after at the most three steps, is restarted into a canter with the other leg leading with no steps at the trot.

Changes of Direction:
1. At changes of direction the horse should adjust the bend of his body to the curvature of the line he follows remaining supple and following the indications of the rider without any resistance or change of pace, rhythm or speed.
2. When changing direction at right angles, for instance when riding corners, the horse

should be correctly bent and balanced, ridden as deeply as is appropriate to its level of training, into the corner.
3. When changing direction in form of counter-change of hand the rider changes direction by moving obliquely either to the quarter line or in the center line or to the opposite long side of the arena whence he returns on an oblique line to the line he was following when he started the movement.
4. At the counter-change of hand the rider should make his horse straight an instant before changing direction. When for instance at counter-change of hand at half-pass to either side of the center line the number of meters or strides to either side is prescribed in the test, it must be strictly observed and the movement be executed symmetrically.

(Article 1909, AHSA Rulebook 1992-93)

Collection:
1. The aim of the collection of the horse is:
   a) To further develop and improve the balance and equilibrium of the horse which has been more or less displaced by the additional weight of the rider.
   b) To develop and increase the horse's ability to lower and engage his quarters for the benefit of the lightness and mobility of his forehand.
   c) To add to the "ease and carriage" of the horse and to make him more pleasurable to ride.
2. The best means to obtain these aims are the lateral movements, travers, renvers and, last but not least, shoulder-in, as well as half-halts.
3. Collection is, in other words, improved and effected by engaging the hind legs with the joints bent and supple, forward under the horse's body by a temporary but often repeated action of the seat and legs of the rider driving the horse forward towards a more or less stationary or restraining hand allowing just enough impulsion to pass through. Collection is consequently not achieved by shortening of the pace through a resisting action of the hand but instead by using the seat and legs to engage the

hindlegs further under the horse's body.

4. However, the hindlegs should not be engaged too far forward under the horse as this would shorten the base of support too much and thereby impede the movement. In such a case, the line of the back would be lengthened and raised in relation to the supporting base of the legs, the stability would be deranged and the horse would have difficulty in finding a harmonious and correct balance.

5. On the other hand, a horse with a too long base of support unable or unwilling to engage his hindlegs forward under his body will never achieve an acceptable collection characterized by ease and carriage as well as a lively impulsion, originated in the activity of the quarters.

6. The position of the head and neck of a horse at the collected paces is naturally dependent on the stage of training and in some degree on his conformation. It should, however, be distinguished by the neck being raised unrestrained forming a harmonious curve from the withers to the poll being the highest point with the head slightly in front of the vertical. However, at the moment the rider applies his aids in order to obtain a momentary and passing collecting effect the head may become more or less vertical.

   (Article 1915, AHSA Rulebook 1992-93)

Curb bit: A bit with shanks and a chin strap whose action is indirect; a one-handed bit.

Donkey: The domestic ass.

Dropped noseband: A cavesson that fastens around the nose below the bit.

Farrier: Horse or mule shoer.

Figures:
1. Serpentine. The first loop is started by moving gradually away from the middle of the short side of the arena and the last loop is finished by moving gradually towards the middle of the opposite short side. Starting and finishing by riding into the corners is incorrect.

2. Figure of eight. This figure consists of two exact voltes or circles of equal size as prescribed in the test joined at the center of the eight. The rider should make his horse straight an instant before changing direction at the center of the figure.

   (Article 1910, AHSA Rulebook 1992-93)

Foal: A baby equine under six months of age.

Flying lead changes: Changes of lead made through the canter.

Gait: A sequence of foot movements by which an equine moves forward.

Gymkhana: Equine games such as barrel racing, pole bending,etc.

Hacking: To ride or drive at an ordinary pace or over the roads as distinguished from racing or riding across country.

Half-Halt: The half-halt is a hardly visible, almost simultaneous, coordinated action of the seat, the legs and the hand of the rider, with the object of increasing the attention and balance of the horse before the execution of several movements or transitions to lesser and higher paces. In shifting slightly more weight onto the horse's quarters, the engagement of the hind legs and the balance on the haunches are facilitated for the benefit of the lightness of the forehand and the horse's balance as a whole. (Article 1908, AHSA Rulebook 1992-93)

Halt:
1. At the halt, the horse should stand attentive, motionless and straight with the weight evenly distributed over all four legs being by pairs abreast with each other. The neck should be raised, the poll high and the head slightly in front of the vertical. While remaining on the bit and maintaining a light and soft contact with the rider's hand, the horse may quietly chomp the bit and should be ready to move off at the slightest indication of the rider.

2. The halt is obtained by the displacement of

the horse's weight on the quarters by a properly increased action of the seat and legs of the rider driving the horse toward a more and more restraining but allowing hand causing an almost instantaneous but not abrupt halt at a previously fixed place.

(Article 1902, AHSA Rulebook 1992-93)

Hame: One or two curved supports which are attached to the collar of the harness to which the traces are fastened.

Harness: Apparatus used to connect the animal to a vehicle.

Hinny: Hybrid cross between a male horse called a stallion and a female donkey called a jennet.

Horse mule, john mule: The male mule.

Hotwalker: A mechanical device used to walk usually four animals at once.

Hot wires: Electrical fence wires.

Impulsion: Impetus; compelling forward motion.

Jack: The male donkey.

Jennet, Jenny: The female donkey.

Lateral movements: Diagonal movements.

Lateral movements:
1. The aim of the lateral movement is:
   a) To improve the obedience of the horse to the cooperative aids of the rider;
   b) To supple all parts of the horse thereby increasing the freedom of his shoulders and the suppleness of his quarters as well as the elasticity of the bond connecting the mouth, the poll, the neck, the back and the haunches;
   c) To improve the cadence and bring the balance and pace into harmony.
   d) To develop and increase the engagement of the quarters and thereby also the collection.
2. At all lateral movements—with the exception of leg-yielding in which the horse is bent only at the pull—the horse is slightly bent and moves with the fore hand and the quarters on two different tracks.
3. As all bending of flexion at the poll and neck has a repercussion on the whole spine, the bend of flexion must never be exaggerated so that it impairs the balance and fluency of the movement concerned; this applies especially to the half-pass where the bend should be less evident than in the shoulder-in, travers and renvers.
4. At the lateral movements the pace should remain free and regular, maintained by a constant impulsion yet it must be supple, cadenced and balanced. The impulsion is often lost because of the rider's preoccupation mainly in bending the horse and pushing him sideways.
5. Lateral movements should only be practiced for a relatively short time, now and then interrupted by some energetic movement straight forward, inter alia in order to maintain or increase the impulsion.
6. At all lateral movements the side to which the horse should be bent is the inside. The opposite side is the outside.
7. The lateral movements comprise: leg-yielding, shoulder-in, travers (head to the wall), renvers (tail to the wall) and half-pass.

(Article 1911, AHSA Rulebook 1992-93)

Leg-yielding: The horse is quite straight except for a slight bend at the poll so that the rider is just able to see the eyebrow and nostril on the inside. The inside legs pass and cross in front of the outside legs. The horse is looking away from the direction in which he is moving. Leg-yielding is the most basic of all lateral movements and should be included in the training of the horse before he is ready for collected work. Later on, together with the more advanced movement shoulder-in, it is the best means of making a horse supple, loose and unconstrained for the benefit of the freedom, elasticity and regularity of his paces and the harmony, lightness and ease of his movements. Leg-yielding can be performed on the diagonal in which case the horse should be as close as possible parallel to the long sides of the arena although the forehand should be slightly in advance of the quarters. It can also be performed along the wall in which case the horse should be at an angle of about 35 degrees to the direction in which he is moving.

Shoulder-in: The horse is slightly bent round the inside leg of the rider. The horse's inside foreleg passes and crosses in front of the outside leg, the inside hind leg is placed in front of the outside leg. The horse is looking away from the direction in which he is moving. Shoulder-in if performed in the right way with the horse slightly bent round the inside leg of the rider and at the correct angle, is not only a suppling movement but also a collecting movement. The horse at every step must move his inside hindleg underneath his body and place it in front of the outside which he is unable to do without lowering his inside hip. Shoulder-in is performed along the wall at an angle of about 30 degrees to the direction in which the horse is moving.

Lead: The front leg the animal leads with in the canter determines what lead he is on.

Lead line: Lead rope; any line that is attached to the halter and used to pull the animal along.

Lunge line: Usually a twenty-five foot rope or nylon strap used for circling the animal around you during exercise.

Molly mule: The female mule.

Mule: Hybrid cross between a male donkey called a jack and a female horse called a mare.

Negative reinforcement: A negative reward for a behavior; punishment.

Pleasure class: A flat class where animals are asked to show at the walk, at the trot, at the canter and backing.

Plumb line: Exactly vertical or true line.

Poll: The top of the equine's head between the ears.

Positive reinforcement: A positive reward for a behavior; treat.

Reinback: Backing, back-up.

Rein Back:
1. The rein back is an equilateral, retrograde movement in which the feet are raised and set down almost simultaneously by diagonal pairs, each forefoot being raised and set down an instant before the diagonal hind foot so that on hard ground sometimes four separate beats are clearly audible. The feet should be well raised and the hind feet remain well in line.
2. At the preceding halt as well as during the rein back the horse, although standing motionless and moving backwards respectively, should remain on the bit maintaining his desire to move forward.
3. Anticipation or precipitation of the movement, resistance to or evasion of the hand, deviation of the quarters from the straight line, spreading or inactive hind legs and dragging forefeet are serious faults.
4. If in a dressage test a trot or canter is required after a rein back the horse should move off immediately into this pace without a halt or an intermediate step.
   (Article 1906, AHSA Rulebook 1992-93)

Reining: A class in which the animal exhibits that he is willfully guided or controlled with little or no apparent resistance and dictated to completely.

Rhythm: Movement of fluctuation marked by the regular reoccurrence or natural flow of related elements.

Seatbones: Two prominent bones in the pelvis that you sit upon.

Shafts: Two long pieces of wood between which an equine is hitched to a vehicle.

Shank: A chain used for halter showing and stallion management.

Sidepass: A movement in which the equine moves directly sideways.

Simple lead changes: Changes of lead made through the trot.

Sliding stop: A stop in reining where the animal slides on the back feet while walking with the front feet.

Snaffle bit: A bit whose action comes directly from the corners of the mouth; a direct rein bit.

Spin: A 360-degree or more turn on the haunches as done in reining.

Submission:

1. Submission does not mean a truckling subservience but an obedience revealing its presence by a constant attention, willingness and confidence in the whole behavior of the horse as well as by the harmony, lightness and ease he is displaying in the execution of the different movements. The degree of submission is also manifested by the way the horse accepts the bridle; with a light and soft contact, a supple poll or with resistance to or evasion of the rider's hand; being either above the bit or behind the bit respectively.

2. Putting out the tongue, keeping it above the bit or drawing it up altogether as well as grinding teeth and swishing the tail are mostly signs of nervousness, tenseness or resistance on the part of the horse and must be taken into account by the judges in their marks for the movement concerned as well as in the collective mark for submission. (Article 1916, AHSA Rulebook 1992-93)

Surcingle: A belt, band, or girth passing around the body of the animal.

Transitions:

1. The changes of pace and speed should be clearly shown at the prescribed marker; they should be quickly made yet must be smooth and not abrupt. The cadence of a pace should be maintained up to the moment when the pace is changed or the horse halts. The horse should remain light in hand, calm and maintain a correct position.

2. The same applies to transitions from one movement to another for instance from the passage to the piaffe and vice versa.
(Article 1907, AHSA Rulebook 1992-93)

Trot:

1. The trot is a pace of "two time" on alternate diagonal legs (near left fore and right hind leg and vice versa) separated by a moment of suspension.

2. The trot, always with free, active and regular steps, should be moved into without hesitation.

3. The quality of the trot is judged by the general impression, the regularity and elasticity of the steps—originated from a supple back and well engaged hindquarters—and by the ability of maintaining the same rhythm and natural balance even after a transition from one trot to another.

4. The following trots are recognized: working trot, collected trot, medium trot, and extended trot.

5. All trot work is executed sitting unless otherwise indicated in the test concerned.
(Article 1904, AHSA Rulebook 1992-93)

Collected trot: The horse remaining on the bit moves forward with his neck raised and arched. The hocks being well engaged maintain an energetic impulsion thus enabling the shoulders to move with greater ease in any direction. The horse's steps are shorter than in the other trots but he is lighter and more mobile.

Extended trot: The horse covers as much ground as possible. Maintaining the same cadence he lengthens his steps to the utmost as a result of great impulsion from the hindquarters. The rider allows the horse remaining on the bit without leaning on it to lengthen his frame and to gain ground. The forefeet should touch the ground on the spot towards which they are pointing. The whole movement should be well balanced and the transition to collected trot should be smoothly executed by taking more weight on the hindquarters.

Medium trot: This is a pace between the working and the extended trot but more "round" than the latter. The horse goes forward with free and moderately extended steps and an obvious impulsion from the hindquarters. The rider allows the horse remaining on the bit to carry his head a little more in front of the vertical than at the collected and the working trot and allows him at the same time to lower his head and neck slightly. The steps should be as even as possible and the whole movement balanced and unconstrained.

Working trot: This is a pace between the collected and the medium trot in which a horse not yet trained and ready for collected movements shows himself properly balanced and, remaining on the bit, goes forward with even, elastic steps and good hock action. The expression "good hock action" does not mean that collection is a required quality of Working trot. It only underlines the importance of an impulsion originating from the activity of the hindquarters.

Tug: Trace.

Turn-on-the-forehand: This movement is a schooling exercise which can be executed from the halt or walk. The equine's hindquarters move in even, quiet and regular steps around the equine's inside front leg while maintaining the rhythm of the walk. Backing or losing rhythm are considered a serious fault.

Turn-on-the-haunches: This movement is a schooling exercise which can be executed from a halt or walk and is preparatory for the pirouette which is executed out of a collected gait. The horse's forehand moves in even, quiet and regular steps around the horse's inner hind leg while maintaining the rhythm of the walk. In the half turn on the haunches the horse is not required to step with its inside hind leg in the same spot each time it leaves the ground but may move slightly forward. Backing or loss of rhythm are considered a serious fault. This movement may be executed through 90 degrees, 180 degrees, or 360 degrees.

(Article 1912, AHSA Rulebook 1992-93)

Vigor: Active bodily or mental strength.

Walk:

1. The walk is a marching pace in which the footfalls of the horse's feet follow one another in "four time," well marked and maintained in all work at the walk.

2. When the four beats cease to be distinctly marked, even and regular the walk is disunited or broken.

3. It is at the pace of walk that the imperfections of Dressage are most evident. This is also the reason why a horse should not be asked to walk on the bit at the early stages of his training. A too precipitous collection will not only spoil the collected walk but the medium and the extended walk as well.

4. The following walks are recognized: working walk, collected walk, medium walk, extended walk, and free walk.

(Article 1903, AHSA Rulebook 1992-93)

Collected walk: The horse remaining on the bit moves resolutely forward with his neck raised and arched. The head approaches the vertical position, the light contact with the mouth being maintained. The hind legs are engaged with good hock action. The pace should remain marching and vigorous, the feet being placed in regular sequence. Each step covers less ground and is higher than at the medium walk because all the joints bend more markedly. The hind feet touch the ground behind or at most, in the footprints of the forefeet. In order not to become hurried or irregular the collected walk is shorter than the medium walk, although showing greater activity.

Extended walk: The horse covers as much ground as possible without haste and without losing the regularity of his steps, the hind feet touching the ground clearly in front of the footprints of the forefeet. The rider allows the horse to stretch out his head and neck without, however, losing contact with the mouth.

Free walk: The free walk is a pace of relaxation in which the horse is allowed complete freedom to lower and stretch out his head and neck. Free Walk on a Long Rein: Freedom to lower and

stretch out his head and neck while still maintaining contact.
Free Walk on a Loose Rein: Riding the buckle.

Medium walk: A free, regular and unconstrained walk of moderate extension. The horse remaining on the bit walks energetically but calmly with even and determined steps, the hind feet touching the ground in front of the footprints of the forefeet. The rider maintains a light but steady contact with the mouth.

Working walk: A regular and unconstrained walk. The horse should walk energetically but calmly with even and determined steps with distinctly marked four equally spaced beats. The rider should maintain a light and steady contact with the horse's mouth.

Way of going: The equine's way of moving.

Weanling: A young equine who is under one year of age and is no longer nursing.

Yearling: An equine who is one year of age.

References

Organizations

American Donkey & Mule Society
Paul and Betsy Hutchins
2901 North Elm Street
Denton, Texas 76201

American Driving Society/Rocky
Mountain Carriage Club
11000 Highway 34 Bypass
Greeley, Colorado 80631

American Trakehner Horse Association
1520 West Church Street
Newark, Ohio 43055

British Mule Society
Lorraine Travis
Hope Mount Farm, Top of Hope
Alstonfield, Nr. Ashbourne
Derbyshire, DE6 2FR, Great Britain

The Donkey Sanctuary
Sidmouth, Devon
EX10 ONU, Great Britain

International Side Saddle Organization
PO Box 282
Alton Bay, New Hampshire 03810

United States Dressage Federation
1212 O Street
PO Box 80668
Lincoln, Nebraska 68501

United States Combined Training
Association
292 Bridge Street
South Hampton, Massachusetts 01982

Books

American Horse Shows Association Rule
Book 1992-1993
220 East 42nd Street
New York, New York 10017-5876

Centered Riding
by Sally Swift
A Trafalgar Square Farm Book
David & Charles, Inc.
North Pomfret, Vermont 05053

*The Complete Training of Horse and
Rider*
by Alois Podhasky
Library of Congress catalog card #67-
11157
English Translation — 1967 by Doubleday
& Co., Inc.

A Winning Way
Richard Schrake
PO Box 4490
Sunriver, Oregon 97707

Magazines

Dressage & C.T.
1772 Middlehurst Road
Cleveland Heights, Ohio 44118-1648

Driving Digest magazine
PO Box 467
Brooklyn, Connecticut 06234

Driving West magazine
PO Box 2675
Chino, California 91708

Equus magazine
656 Quince Orchard Road
Gaithersburg, Maryland 20878

Horseplay magazine
11 Park Avenue
PO Box 130
Gaithersburg, Maryland 20884

Mules and More magazine
Rt. 1, Box 269
Bland, Missouri 65014

About the Author

Meredith Hodges, born in Minneapolis, Minnesota, and raised in California, has been associated with mules and donkeys for eighteen years and has been associated with horses all of her life. She worked as assistant trainer for the Windy Valley Mule Ranch in Healdsburg, California, until its dispersal in 1979, at which time she started the Lucky Three Mule Ranch in Loveland, Colorado, with selected Windy Valley broodstock. Since, she has studied Animal Sciences at Colorado State University; she is an animal inspector, representative, and judge for the American Donkey and Mule Society; and, she's had a successful column called Mule Crossing appear in over ten different publications internationally for more than eight years. She sponsors Longears research at Colorado State and Louisiana State universities. Always working toward the positive promotion of Longears, Meredith has studied horsemanship with a variety of instructors and clinicians, including world-class jumping instructor Denny Emerson and Swedish Olympic Team member Major Anders Lindgren. Melinda Weatherford, USDF/USCTA regional instructor, sees to it that Meredith is continually learning more with two lessons a week regularly. Meredith got mules accepted by the USDF in 1986, and in 1988, she and three of her mules appeared in the Tournament of Roses parade held in Pasadena on New Year's Day. After successfully competing in breed shows for several years, Meredith further challenged her mules to compete in Dressage and Combined Training. Today they excel beyond what anyone would have expected! Meredith also trained Little Jack Horner, the only formal jumping donkey in the world today! Meredith's Lucky Three Ranch is known throughout the world for its excellence in the production and promotion of top quality, athletic saddle mules and donkeys!

Index

A

Abbe Ranch, 179
affection, toward mule, 33, 103
affectionate attitude, of jack, 11
age of specialization, 203
aggressiveness
    of jack, 11
    of mules, 27
aids, 4, 173. See also separate
    listings for each type of aid
    clarification of, 133-137
    fine tuning of, 177-179
    meaning of, 161
    responsiveness to, 178
    when the rider asks with aids,
        161
Altieri, Gail, 75, 175
American Donkey and Mule
    Society, 12
appropriateness, of animal to
    vehicle, 94
arm position, of rider, 175
assessment, of mule's strong
    points, 66
assistant, when to use, 87, 99-101
athletic ability, of mule, 1
athletics, equine, 65, 111
attentiveness, how to
    cultivate, 27
attitudes
    and use of restraints, 181-187
    of the trainer, 181
avoidance behavior, 6

B

baby oil, for highlighting, 193
"Back" command, 7, 61, 113
backing up, 68, 104, 127, 160, 178
    See also long line rein back
"bad hands," 175
balance, 97, 99, 119, 136, 137, 162,
    165
    better balance and lateral
        response, 153-157
    correcting, 178
    facilitating, 139-145
    lateral, 121
    loss of, 167
    on the reins, 174
    problems with, 121
    shifting, 177
    vertical, 165
balancing, in half-halt, 73
Banks, Jerry, 200, 204
bathing, 189
"behind" the legs, 161
belligerence, of jack, 11
bend, and forward movement,
    121
bending
    correct, 140
    exercises, 67
Bishop Mule Days, 128, 135, 136,
    188, 193
bits
    broken-mouth snaffle, 59
    release of as reward, 61

bits (continued)
    training, 59
Bitterroot Mule Company, 10
bitting, 52-53, 59
Blue Zebulon, 10, 132
body language, 171, 172
body mechanics, 127
body movements, 9
    coordination of rider's with
        mule's, 133, 166
body position, of rider, 177
body shifts, 9, 155
books, list of, 215
boredom, avoiding, 140
borium shoes, 204
braiding
    of foretop, 192, 198
    of mane, 192, 194-197
    of tail, 192, 199
brakes, for breaking carts, 87
brand inspection, 189
Brayer Hill mules and donkeys
    Bubba, 191
    Eagle Rest Don Quixote, 92, 191
    Razzle Dazzle, 21
breaking carts, 87
breast collar, 79
breeching, 79, 80, 82, 97, 129, 207
breeding, 11-12
bridges, as obstacles, 66
bridle, 39
    putting on, 52, 79, 84, 85
bridle path, 202

British Mule Society, 100
bucking, 59, 101

C
cadence, 121, 159, 165, 207
call to balance, 115
canter
    collected, 207
    description of, 114, 207
    fextended, 207
    lengthened, 165
    medium, 207
    working, 207
canter circle exercise, 115,
    118-119
"Canter" command, 7, 113
canter spiral, 156
canter to trot, 49, 109
carts, 87-91
catching
    difficult mules, 27-29
    mule foal, 20
cavaletti, 66, 141-142, 144, 145,
    147, 159
cavesson, 63
center of gravity, 173, 177
change of direction, 76, 77, 208
change of leg at canter, simple,
    208
change of leg in the air, 208
change of leg through the trot,
    207-208
"chase" game of, 21
chest, of mule, 1
cinching up, 59
circle at the trot, 57
circles, 66, 109, 139
    balanced, 154
    enlarging laterally, 154
cleaning, of tack, 190
Clearview Farms, 134, 154
clipping, for show, 189-199
    procedures for, 192-193
    when to do, 192
clothing, changes for show,
    190-191
Coggins testing, 189
collar, 79, 82, 83, 84
collected trot, 94
collection, 208-209
Colorado Classic Horse Show,
    110, 132, 190

communication
    with the mule, 160
    with the vet and farrier, 203
concentration, sign of in mules,
    21
conditioners, 193
conditioning
    of the mule, 93, 94, 153-159
    programs, 140
    through balance, 113-119
cones, use of, 66, 114-115, 116-
    117, 118 119, 122, 125, 147 151,
    161-162
confidence, of mule in trainer, 40,
    171, 201
consistency, in training, 34, 39
control
    and vertical balance, 165
    of donkeys, 5
coordination, of hand and whip
    cues, 74
corn oil, 189
corrals, for training, 65
counterbend, 159
counter-canter, 208
cow work, 160
crops, use of in training, 6, 133
    135
crossing diagonals, 74, 77
crupper, 53, 63, 79, 80, 81
cues
    leg and seat, 121, 133, 139
    subtle, 139
curb bit, 209
curb chain, 85
curry comb, 102, 193

D
dam, importance of in foal's
    behavior, 27
dandy brush, 192, 193
depth perception, of equines, 34-
    35, 127
desensitization, 202
diagonals, 154, 169
direction, change of. See
    "Reverse"
"direction," of rider's legs, 154
directions, receiving from
    mule's back, 99
disciplinary tactics, 201
disposition, of donkeys, 3

dominance, assertion of, 171
donkeys
    clubs for, 3
    control of, 5
    definition of, 209
    differences between donkeys
        and mules, 5
    farms for, 3
    training of, 6-9
    understanding, 5-9
draw reins
    as a restraint, 182, 184
    settings for, 187
    use of in training, 6, 7, 63
dress, for driving class, 97
dressage, 107-111
    training-level, 109
dress rehearsals, for show, 190
Dr. Feelgood, 172
drilling, improper use of, 7
driving
    behind a cart, 90
    the cart, 91
driving class, 93-94
driving lines, 60
driving mules, judging, 93-97
driving poles, 89
dropped noseband, 209
ducking out, 178

E
"earing-down," 192
ears, laying back of, 21
ears, of the mule, 84, 93
elbow pull, 54-55, 60, 184, 187
Elkins, Ruth, 180
emotional needs, of young
    mules, 171
encouragement, for backing up,
    128
Europe, and equestrian arts, 153
evasiveness, reasons for, 27
exposure, of young mules to
    humans, 165
extended trot, while driving a
    cart, 91
extension, 26
eye position, of rider, 174, 178

F
"Face me" command, 28
face tie, 186

false canter, 208
false martingale, 82
farrier, 209
    complaints about, 203
    responsibilities to, 201-205
fatigue, preventing, 155
feeding schedules, 15
feet
    cleaning, 31
    control of foal's, 20
fence lines, 44, 121
fencing, 11
"fencing," exercise, 160
figure-eights, 66, 209
figures, 209
"finished" mule, 162
finishing, of the driving mule, 87-91
finish-training, 173
floating, of teeth, 205
Florida State Fair, 108
flying change of leg, 208
flying lead changes, 209
foals, mule, 15-17, 209
    attention span of, 33
    catching, 20
    emotional needs of, 15, 171
    formal training of, 16
    grooming of, 23
    halter training of, 19-21
    likes and dislikes of, 16
    teaching to lead, 19
    weanlings, 20
food, importance of, 9
footwork, 160
foretop, braiding of, 192, 198
"Forward" exercises, 87
forward/lateral connection,
    clarification of, 159-163
forward motion
    and correct backing, 160
    inhibition of, 114
    learning, 121
    rider-controlled, 147
    self-balancing, 147
frame, proper, 114, 122
friendship, development of
    between mule and trainer, 171
frustration, avoiding, 140, 155, 181

G
gaits, 60, 114, 209

games, 16
"gates," of cones, 161-162
"Gee" command, 7, 62, 74, 113
"Gee-around" command, 7
"Gee-over" command, 7
George Riding Club (South
    Africa), 111
goal definition, for training, 114
grooming
    for show, 189-199
    of mule foals, 23
ground-driving, 6, 104
    in the open, 65-71
    in the round pen, 59-63
    patterns, 66
ground manners, 7, 19-23
ground poles, 70, 140, 141, 142,
    143, 145, 147, 155, 159
ground-work, 7
    for training to saddle, 99
gymkhana, 209
gymnastics exercises, 140-142,
    159, 165, 173

H
hacking, 209
half-halt, 73, 74, 115, 148, 154,
    159, 162, 165, 179, 209
halt, 8, 47, 61, 209
halt squarely on the lead, 39
halters, show, 189
halter training
    as basic training, 39-40
    of mule foals, 17, 19-22
    of the jack, 12
hames, 79, 83, 210
handler, use of, 203
hand position
    as an aid, 161
    for driving, 97
    for riding, 140
hanging, off the saddle, 99
happiness, 3
hard hat, when to use, 87
harmony, facilitating, 139-145,
    173
harness, 210
    adjusting, 79-85
    how to harness the mule, 79
    in a driving class, 97
"Haw" command, 7, 62, 73, 74, 113
"Haw-around" command, 7

"Haw-over" command, 7
head carriage, 65
head set, 140
headstall, 59
health, concern for by donkeys,
    3
helmet, when to use, 87
hesitation, 133
high-headedness, 65
highlighters, artificial, 189, 193
hind feet, restraining, 183
hindquarter engagement,
    enhancing, 166
hindquarters, of mule, 1
hinny, 210
hitching up, the mule, 87
hobbles, 182, 184, 202
Hodges, Dena, 28, 94, 120, 176,
    202, 203
Hodges, Gary, 88, 106, 110, 164
Hodges, Meredith, 38, 86, 94, 98,
    106, 110, 111, 112, 126, 128, 134,
    135, 138, 141, 146, 154, 158,
    162, 164, 168, 173, 176, 179, 180,
    188, 190, 203, 216
Hoof black, 193
hoof polishing, 189, 193
horse
    differences between mule and
        horse, 1, 5, 181
    qualities of inherited by mule, 1
horse chutes, for restraint, 202,
    205
horse mule, 210
hot walker, 39, 42, 210
hot wires, for fencing, 11, 210
hourglass pattern, 114-115, 116-
    117, 121, 133, 135, 139, 140,
    147
    circling cones, 122, 125
Howe, Fran, 10, 132
humor, and mule foals, 16

I
impulsion, 210
intelligence, of donkeys, 3

J
jack
    breeding of, 12-13
    care and handling of, 11-13
    dangers of, 13

jack (continued)
  definition of, 210
  mule, 1
  qualities of inherited by mule, 1
jennet, 15, 210
jenny, 210
Joling, Jim, 92
judging, the driving mule, 93-97
jumping, 142, 144, 154

K
kicking, 20, 202
King, Sue, 191
kisses, for mule foals, 25
Knebel, K. M., 205
knees, 113

L
lateral control, 8, 66
lateral exercises, 73, 147-151
  on long lines, 73-77
  patterns for teaching, 73-74
lateral movement, 147, 210
lateral response, 165
  and better balance, 153-157
lateral wheel exercise, 122, 124,
    147
lateral work, under saddle, 147-
    151
  most common mistake in, 149
    stressfulness of, 149
    warmup for, 147
lead changes, simple, 212
leading, 7, 12, 19, 24-25, 201, 211
lead line, 211
leaning, on bridle, 6
Lee, Dennis, 191
leg cues, 121, 133, 139, 175
leg, impulsing, 139
legs
  as an aid, 161. See also leg cues
  concept and function of, 153-
    154, 173
  moving off of the, 121-125
  "on," 154
leg yield, 4, 76, 146, 148, 149, 150,
    151, 153-157, 210-211
lengthened canter, 165
lengthened trot, 165, 169
limitations, physical, 142
lines, straight, as dressage
    pattern, 109

lines, use of, 33
  fighting, 34
  long, 62, 67
  long-line rein back, 68
Lipizzaners, 107
loading, teaching mule to, 33-37
  difficult, 37
  easy, 36
  modified approach, 34
logs, as obstacles, 66
long line obstacles, 70-71
long line rein back, 68
long lines
  lateral work on, 73-77
  side passing on, 74
Lory State Park, 138
Loveland Carriage Classic, 94, 95
Lucky Three mules and donkeys
  Bitterroot Cody, 42
  Bitterroot Spider Dee, 143, 144
  Blue Baron, 13
  Calypso, 30, 31, 40, 43, 50, 52,
    54, 56, 68, 102-103
  Ciji, 2, 75, 80, 86, 126, 142, 150,
    157, 166, 176, 188, 190, 203
  Cyclone, 106, 110
  Desirée, 108
  Eclipse, 57, 164
  Felicia's Fairytale, 18, 21, 26,
    32, 36
  Ferrara, 35
  Firestorm, 17, 38, 98, 106, 111,
    112, 162
  Foxfire, 40, 42, 63, 104
  Jubilee, 23
  Little Jack Horner, 2, 4, 7, 12,
    13, 114, 128, 129, 141, 142,
    148, 174
  Mae Bea C.T., 80, 86, 89, 90, 91,
    94, 95, 96, 110, 120, 136, 138,
    142, 158, 173, 176, 179, 188,
    203
  Mae C.J., 2
  Melinda's Masterpiece (Lindy),
    21, 41, 44, j205
  Mercedes, 16
  Midnight Victory, 14, 72, 101
  Mister Moon, 40
  Moonrocket, 40, 42
  Nuggett, 58, 67, 76
  Pantera, 16, 35
  Rambling Rose, 202

Lucky Three mules and donkeys
(continued)
  Selene, 29
  Serendipity, 8
  Stardust, 64, 88, 96, 154
  Sundowner, 2, 134, 135, 146,
    154, 156, 167, 168, 169
  Twilight, 109
  Vicki, 21
  Vinesse, 14, 101
lunge line, 34, 47, 56-57, 59, 211
  use in training to saddle, 100-
    101
lunging, 6, 58, 59, 165
  free lunging in round pen, 50-51
  in the elbow pull, 54-55
  in the open, 57
  in the round pen, 56
  problems with, 172
  training, 39, 47-57

M
magazines, list of, 215
mailboxes, as obstacles, 66, 70
manageability, of the mule, 201
mane, braiding of, 192, 194-197
manners, of the mule, 93
martingales, 182
maturation, of mules, 113
McElvain, Diane, 111, 155, 170,
    172
menstruation, effect on jacks and
    stallions, 13
mental ability, of mules, 113
mental attitude, 127
molly mule, 211
mounting, 102-105
  first, 42-43
moving away from the leg,
    concept of, 122
mules
  and horses, differences in
    training, 181
  clubs for, 3
  cultivating relationships with,
    171
  differences between mules and
    donkeys, 5
  driving, 87-97
  farms for, 3
  "finished," 162
  foals, 15-17, 19-25, 27-31.

mules (continued)
    maturation rate of, 113
    mental ability of, 113
    old wives' tales about, 201
    teaching to load, 33-37
    two-year-olds, 47
    young mules and posture, 107
muscular development,
    enhancing, 165-169
muscular structure, of mule, 1
    difference between horse and
        mule, 1

N

National Western Stock Show,
    38, 164, 202
negative reinforcement, 5, 181,
    211
nervousness, of the mule, 65
nipping, 20
North Carolina State Fair, 88
nose position, of mule, 179

O

obstacles, 9, 17, 33, 66, 160
    leading the mule over, 40, 41
    long-line, 70-71
    trail, 66, 69, 75
    use of for lateral exercises, 74
old wives' tales, about mules, 201
Ole King Jole, 75, 175
"on the bit," 139, 161
    definition of, 140
organizations, list of, 215
owners, complaints about, 201

P

patience, importance of, 9, 27, 59
patterns
    for conditioning, 114-119
    for driving, 90
    training-level, 108
pens, use of in training, 28, 47
    round pen, 49, 50-51, 59-63, 65,
        105
persistence, importance of, 27
personality, assessment of, 65
physical language, 165
playfulness, of the mule, 65
pleasure class, 211
plumb line, 211
poles, long. See shafts, driving

poles, long (continued)
    poles; ground poles
poll, 211
positive reinforcement, 28, 61,
    171, 181, 211
posture, 60, 97, 107
    equine, 152, 162, 182
Powell, Cindy, 64, 88, 96, 154
praising the mule, 47, 100, 101,
    149, 154, 160, 166
preparation, importance of, 128
pressure cues, 75
psychology, importance of for
    training, 5
punishment, 6, 20, 61, 181
pushiness, of mule, 171
push-relax movement, 148
push-squeeze movement, 148,
    149

R

rail, side passing the, 71
reassurance, for the mule, 100
rein back, 94, 127-131, 211
rein cues, 75, 87
rein indicators, 6
reining, 107, 160, 173, 211
reins, 79
    adjusting, 67
    attaching to bit, 60
    balance on, 174
    for ground-driving, 85
    riding without, 175, 177
relaxation techniques, 104, 110,
    111
repetition, importance of, 34
resistance, 5, 6, 27, 54, 61, 79, 107,
    113, 127, 155
responsiveness, 133, 135
rest, importance of between
    lessons, 147
restraint, learning, 99
restraints, 67
    abuse of, 182
    choosing correct, 183
    phasing out, 182, 183
    use of, 181-187
    using carefully, 182
"Reverse" command, 49, 54, 55,
    60
reverse movement, rider-
    controlled, 147

review, of previous lessons, 65,
    87, 99, 139
rewarding, of good behavior, 6,
    20, 28, 33, 61, 99, 103
rhythm, 211
    and forward movement, 121,
        159, 165
rider, fine tuning of, 171-175
rider-mule communication, 140
riding
    by "seat of the pants," 175
    without reins, 175, 177
rigging, 60, 63
Rose, Judy, 115
rounding, under rider's seat, 127
round pen. See pens
running off, 6, 61, 67, 99

S

saddle position, problems with,
    101
saddles
    dressage, 108-109
    lateral work under, 147-151
    Western, 108-109
saddle training, 39, 99-105
saddling, 52-53
scotch hobble, 183, 185, 202
scotch rope, 184
scratching, 16, 19, 21
seat bones, 173, 174, 177, 211
seat cues, 121, 135, 139, 159, 161,
    175
security, need for by foals, 15
serpentines, 66, 135, 137, 139, 209
    goals of, 135
shafts, 73, 87, 211
shampoo, for mules, 193
shank, 211
shoeing, 189
shoulder-in, 165, 168, 211
    purpose of, 165
showmanship, 39, 44-45, 165
shying, 66
side passing
    on long lines, 74
    the rail, 71
    the "T," 155, 157
side reins, 57, 148, 182
simple lead changes, 212
slant-loads, 35
sliding stops, 153, 212

snaffle bit, 212
snaffle bridle, 6
"snaky" sensation, 121
snaps, when not to use, 34, 60
social attraction, of donkeys to
    humans, 3
social behavior, of young mules, 3
Spanish Riding School, 107
speed
    and vertical balance, 165
    regulation of, 47
spin, 212
"spooks," 20, 66
spurs, for training, 5, 6, 133, 135
squeeze/release movement, 140,
    148, 159, 160, 177
stability, 66
standing, learning, 70, 201
stiffness, in movement, 178
strains, muscular, 153
strength, enhancing, 165-169
stress, 107, 149
stride, lengthening, 166
stroking, 16, 28, 102
struggling, when loading, 34
stubbornness, 1, 3
submission
    definition of, 212
    learning, 99, 149
surcingle, 59, 79, 80, 82, 212
Sweetwater Laverne, 115

T
tack, 39
    adjustments to, 65
tag, and mule foals, 16
tail, braiding of, 192, 199
talking, to the mule, 41
teamster, in driving class, 97
Tea Party, 155, 170
Temple, Judy, 109
tendons, bowed, 153
Texas State Fair, 172
tie-downs, 182
time, importance of, 11-12
tires, as obstacles, 70
touching, 16, 100, 171, 201
T-poles, 160
trailers
    driving, 35
    loading mule into, 33-37
    preparing for show, 190
    unloading, 35
trail-related exercises, 147

trail riding, for relaxation, 110,
    111, 180
training, basic. See also halter,
    showmanship, lunging,
    trotting, leading, mounting
    beginning, 39-45
    main goal of, 172
    techniques, philosophy
        behind, 171-172
    to saddle, 99-105
training-level patterns, 108
transitions, simple, 109, 212
Travis, Lorraine, 100
treatment, instructions for, 201
treats, use of, 47, 171
trimming, 189
trot
    collected, 212
    description of, 114, 212
    extended, 212
    lengthened, 165, 167, 169
    medium, 213
    posting, 175
    while driving a cart, 91
    working, 213
"Trot" command, 7, 12, 39, 113
"Trot on," 47
trot on the line, 40
trot to canter, 47, 109
trot to walk, 109
trust, importance of in training,
    15, 20, 40, 40, 60, 66, 139
tug, 213
tug, on direct rein, 139
turn-around, 40, 153
turning, aids for, 6
turn on the forehand, 121, 123,
    147, 148, 159, 213
turn on the haunches, 45, 160,
    163, 213
turnout, general, 97
turns, 61
twitch
    chain, 202
    humane, 202
tying off, in trailer, 35

U
United States Dressage
    Federation, 153
unloading, from trailer, 35
"use life," of the mule, 153
Utah State Fair, 98, 106, 111, 112,
    120, 158, 162

V
vaccination, 189
vacuuming the mule, 190
vehicles, for driving class, 95, 97
verbal
    commands, 175
    language, 165
veterinarians
    complaints about, 203
    responsibilities to, 201-205
vigor, 1, 213
visualization, of body move-
    ments, 133

W
walk, 213
    collected, 213
    extended, 213
    free, 213-214
    medium, 214
    working, 214
"Walk" command, 7, 12, 20, 33,
    39, 62, 113
walking
    description of, 114
    exercise, 174
    forward, 60
    in a driving class, 94
    while driving a cart, 91
    with mule foal, 20
walk to halt, 109
walk to trot, 109
water, how to introduce your
    mule to, 30
Watson, Cody Ann, 108
way of going, 94, 214
weaning, 33
weanling, 214
weight, shift of, 174, 177
western pleasure exercises, 147
wheel around, 74
whip, use of in training, 5, 37, 47,
    49, 66, 73-74
"Whoa" command, 6, 12, 39, 47,
    99, 100, 175
worming, 189
working trot, 94
working walk, 174

Y
yearling, 214
yielding
    from center to corner, 148-149, 151
    from corner to center, 148, 151